A-Z PLYM

C000173487

CONTENT

REFERENCE

A Road	A374	Car Park (selected)	P
B Road	B3240	Church or Chapel	†
Dual Carriageway		Cycleway (selected)	🚲
One-way Street		Fire Station	■
Traffic flow on A Roads is also indicated by a heavy line on the driver's left.		Hospital	H
		House Numbers (A & B Roads only)	156 146
Road Under Construction		Information Centre	i
Opening Dates are correct at the time of publication.		National Grid Reference	²45
Proposed Road		Park & Ride	Coypool P+R
Restricted Access		Police Station	▲
Pedestrianized Road		Post Office	★
Track / Footpath		Safety Camera with Speed Limit	(30)
Residential Walkway		Fixed cameras and long term road works cameras Symbols do not indicate camera direction	
Railway	Level Crossing / Station / Tunnel	Toilet: without facilities for the Disabled	▽
		with facilities for the Disabled	▽
		Disabled use only	▽
Built-up Area	BROAD LA	Viewpoint	⁂ ⁂
Local Authority Boundary		Educational Establishment	▢
National Park Boundary		Hospital or Healthcare Building	▢
Posttown Boundary		Industrial Building	▢
Postcode Boundary (within Posttown)		Leisure or Recreational Facility	▢
Map Continuation	14 Large Scale City Centre 5	Place of Interest	▢
		Public Building	▢
		Shopping Centre or Market	▢
Airport	✈	Other Selected Buildings	▢

SCALE

Map Pages 6-38	1:19,000		Map Pages 4-5	1:9,500	
0 ¼ ½ Mile			0 ⅛ ¼ Mile		
0 250 500 750 Metres			0 125 250 375 Metres		
3.33 inches (8.47 cm) to 1 mile 5.26 cm to 1km			6.67 inches (16.94 cm) to 1 mile 10.52 cm to 1km		

Copyright of Geographers' A-Z Map Company Limited

Fairfield Road, Borough Green, Sevenoaks, Kent TN15 8PP
Telephone: 01732 781000 (Enquiries & Trade Sales)
01732 783422 (Retail Sales)
www.az.co.uk
Copyright © Geographers' A-Z Map Co. Ltd.
Edition 6 2014

2 KEY TO MAP PAGES

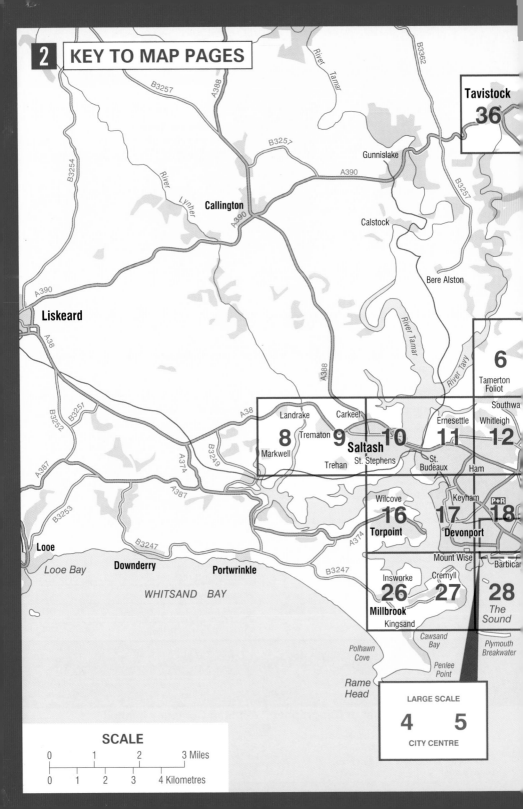

Tavistock 36

River Tamar

B3362

B3257

A388

Gunnislake

A390

B3257

Callington

Calstock

A390

River Lynher

B3254

Bere Alston

River Tamar

Liskeard

A390

A38

A388

River Tavy

6

Tamerton Foliot

A38

Southwa

Landrake   Carkeel

Ernesettle   Whitleigh

8   9   10   11   12

Trematon

Markwell   Saltash

Trehan   St. Stephens   St. Budeaux   Ham

B3252   B3257   A374   B3249   A38

A387

B3253

Wilcove   Keyham

16   17   18   P+R

Torpoint   Devonport

Looe

A374   B3247

Mount Wise   Barbican

Looe Bay   Downderry   Portwrinkle

Insworke   Cremyll

WHITSAND BAY   B3247   26   27   28

Millbrook   The Sound

Kingsand

Polhawn Cove   Cawsand Bay   Plymouth Breakwater

Rame Head   Penlee Point

LARGE SCALE

4   5

CITY CENTRE

SCALE

0   1   2   3 Miles

0   1   2   3   4 Kilometres

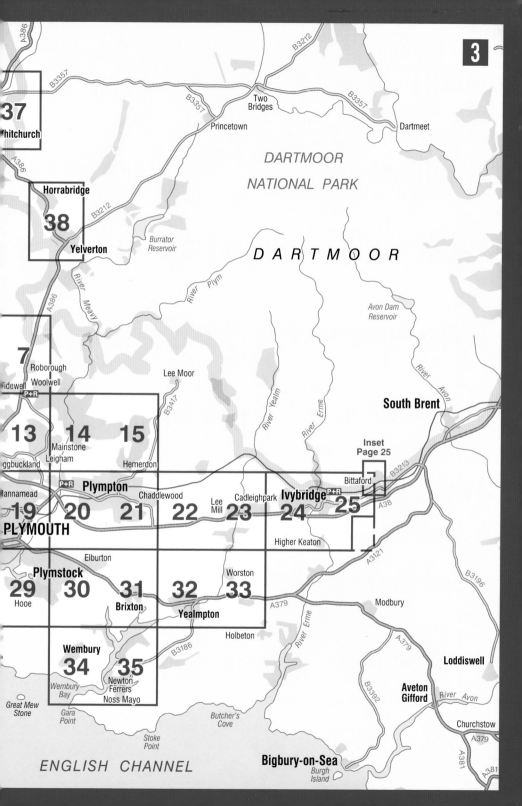

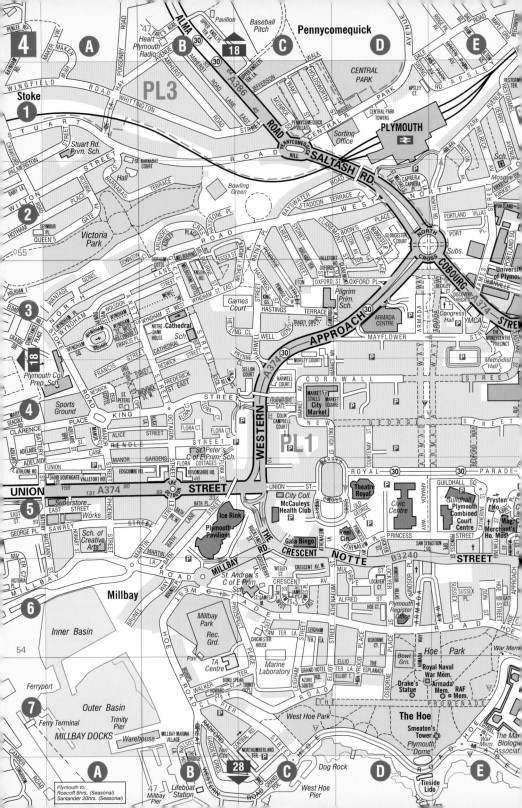

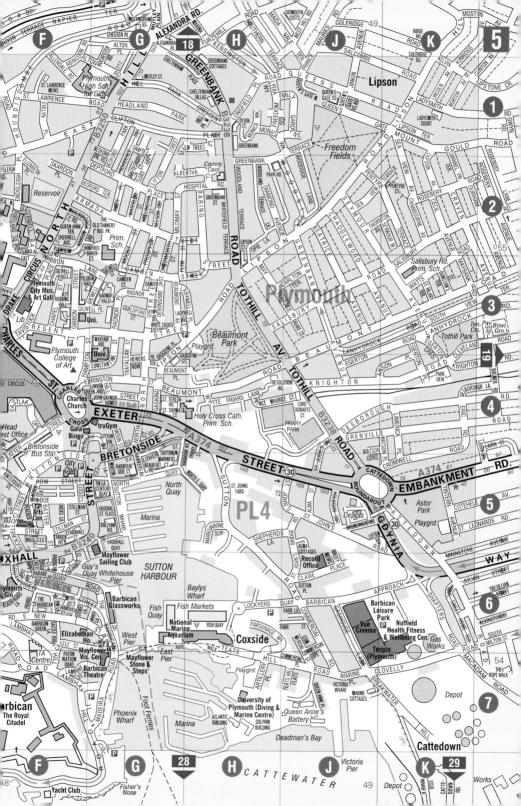

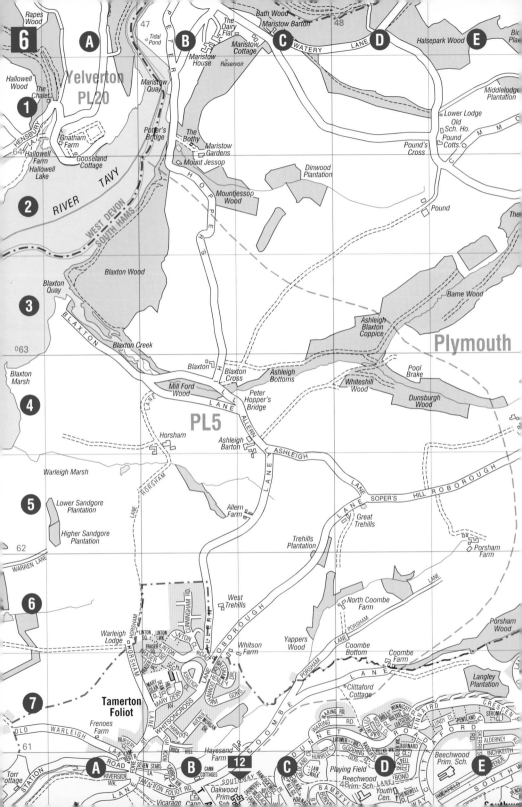

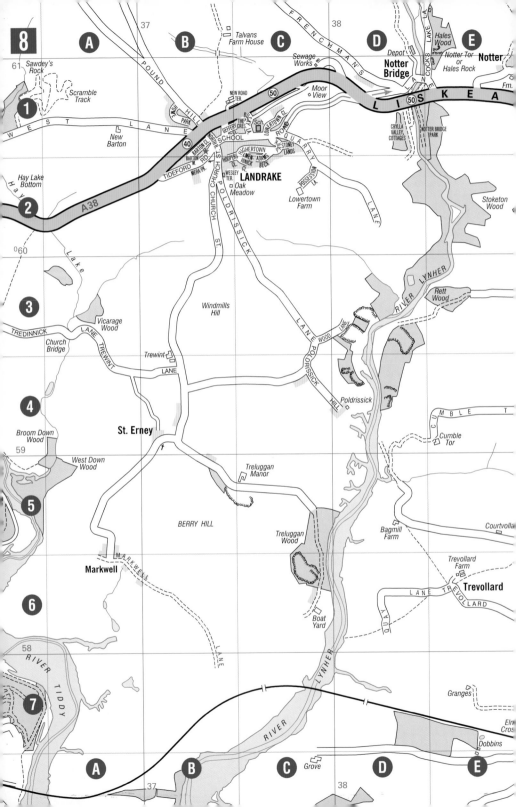

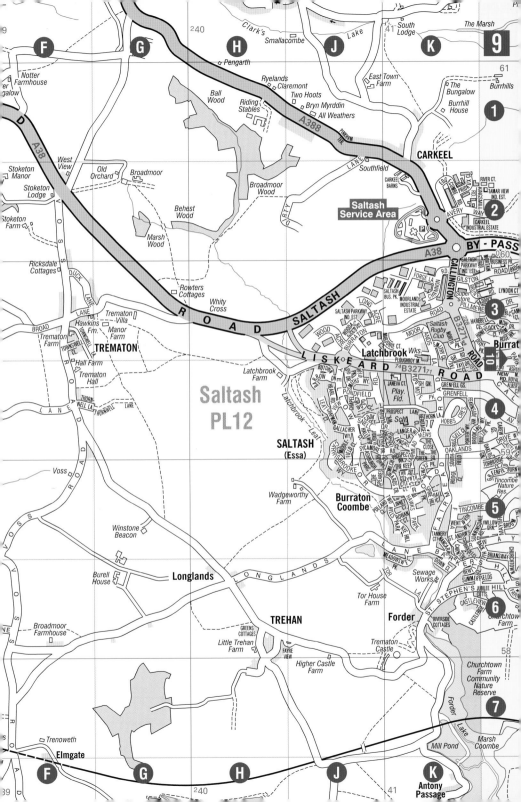

14

A · **B** · **C** · **D** · **E**

Plymouth

Darklake Wood
Henroost Wood
Whittaborough Farm
Brookvi...
Whittaborough Wood
Great Pathill Wood

COMMON WOOD
Ford
Riverford Viaduct
Common Wood Cott.
Common Wood House
Earl's Wood
Hurrabrook Wood
Little Pathill Wood
Little Pethill

DARKLAKE CL.
DARKLAKE VIEW
Works
Works
FORRESTERS BUSINESS PARK
GREAT SHAUGH WOOD
Ramage Wood

Works
Estover Technology Centre
COLWILL WOOD

ESTOVER INDUSTRIAL ESTATE
Weir
PLYMBRIDGE
B4322
Cann Wood Picnic Site

13
Factory
NOVOROSSIYSK RD.
PL6
BICKLEIGH VALE
CANN WOOD

BUSH
PARK
COLWILL WK.
EARLS WOOD
Long Down

COLWILL ROAD
Sub
59 ON 65
HURRABROOK CL.
PATTINSON COURT
PATTINSON
Mainstone

MAINSTONE WOOD
Towers Wood
Plym Bridge Riverside & Woodland Walks
Boringdon Park Wood

PLYMBRIDGE
CRESSBROOK DR.
Plym Bridge
Miners Cottage

Plym Bridge Woods
Plym Bridge Riverside & Woodland Walks
Woodford Wood

BEECHWOOD
WOODLANDS
DRIVE
RISE
LEIGHAM MANOR DR.
MILLWOOD DRIVE

58
Leigham

RIVER PLYM
RIVERSIDE CARAVAN PARK
Shearwood Plantation
Marsh Mills China Clay Works
Triumphal Arch
Hilltops
BORINGDON PARK GOLF COURSE
SOUTH HAMS
PLYMOUTH

Leigham Wood
Toboggan Run
BORINGDON PARK GOLF COURSE
Club House

th Ski Slope
vboard Cen.
Longbridge

A · **B** · **20** · **C** · Woodford · **D** · **E**

CRANFIELD
WOODFORD LA.
LYNMOUTH
BUCKLAND
MEADOW WAY
SOUTH VIEW P...

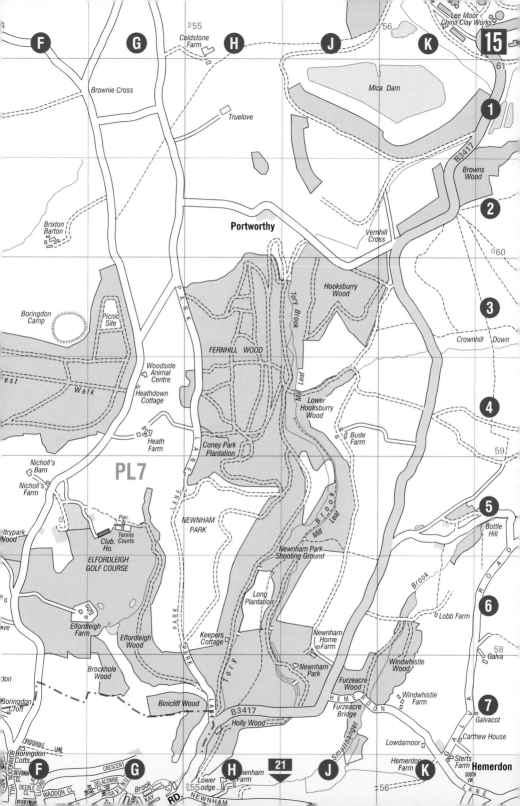

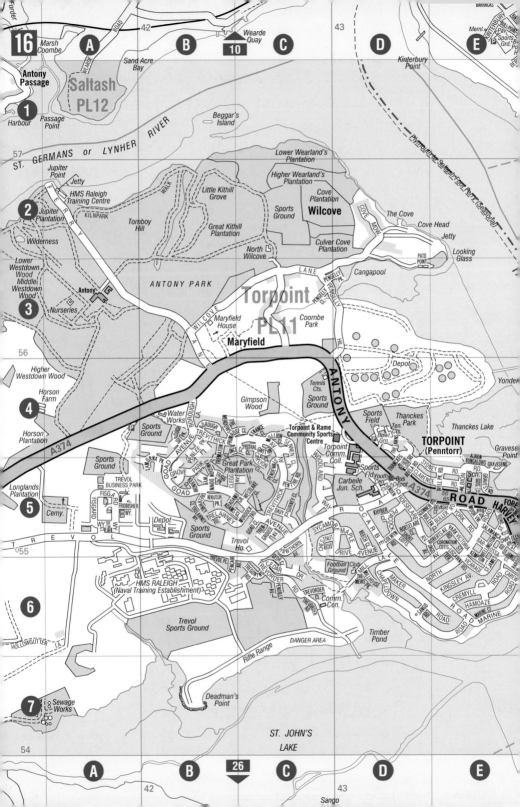

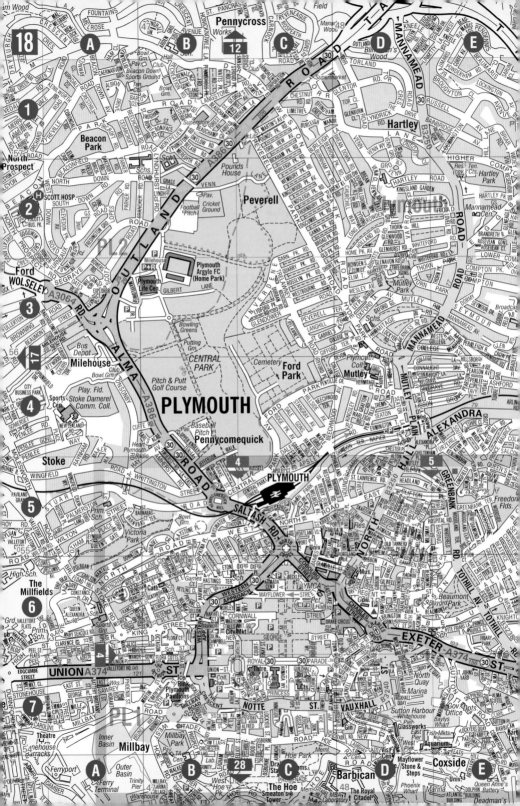

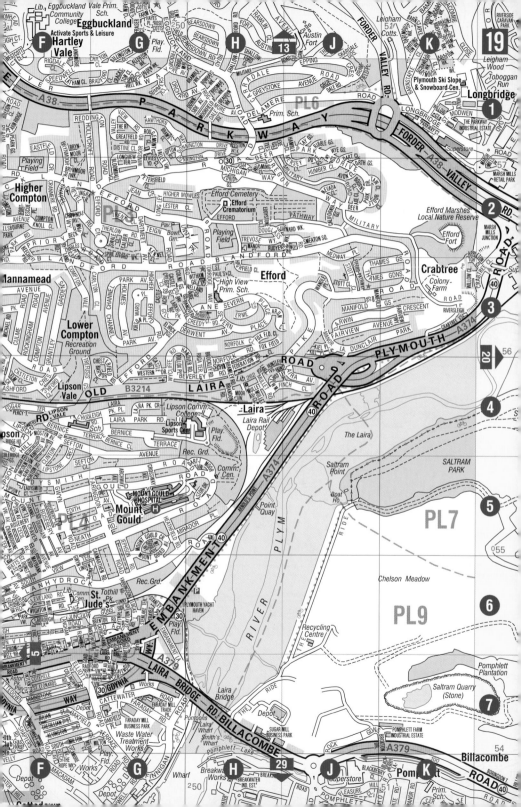

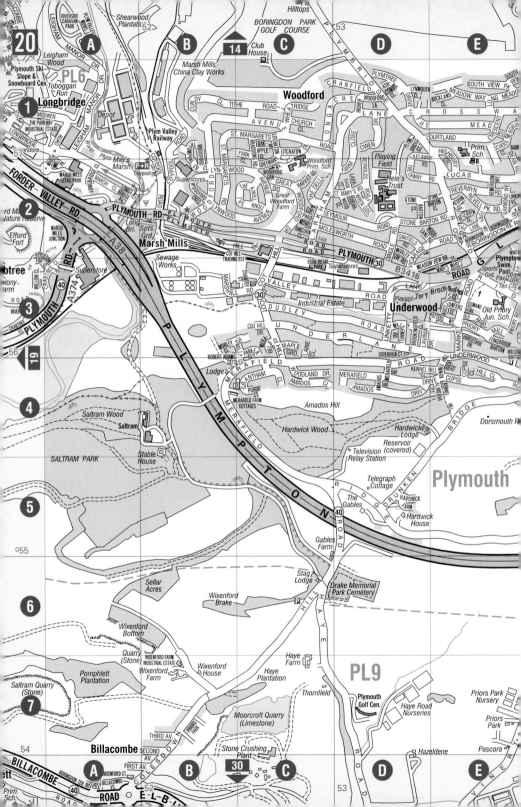

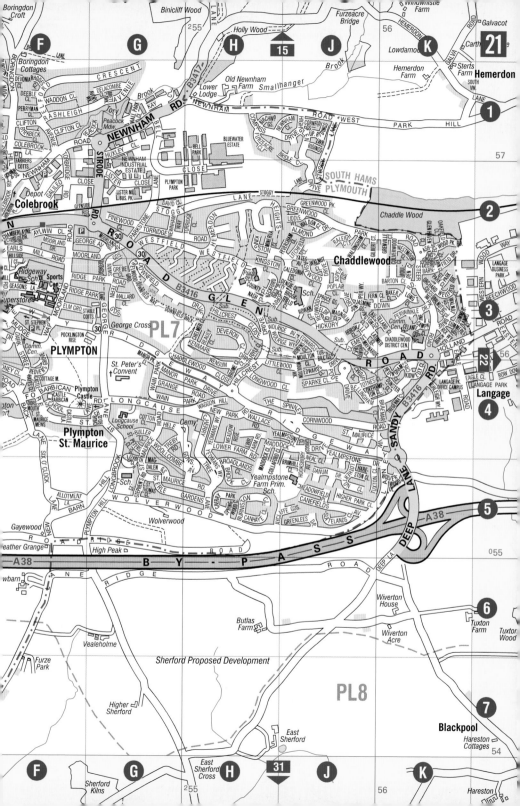

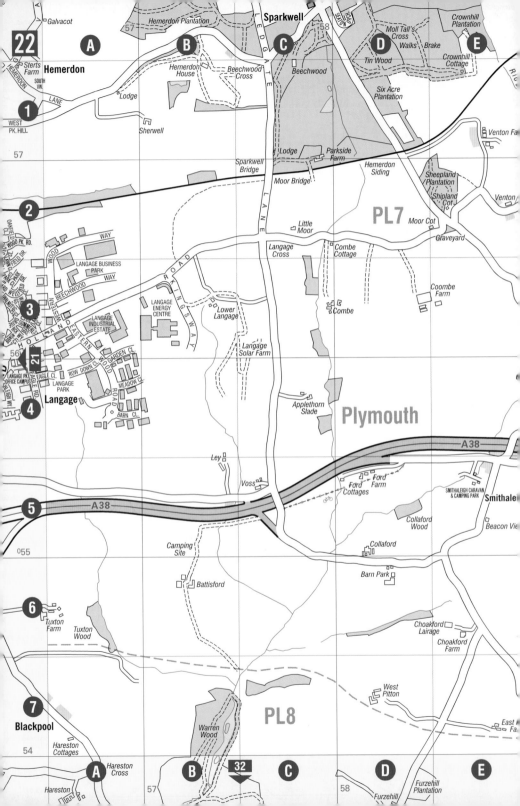

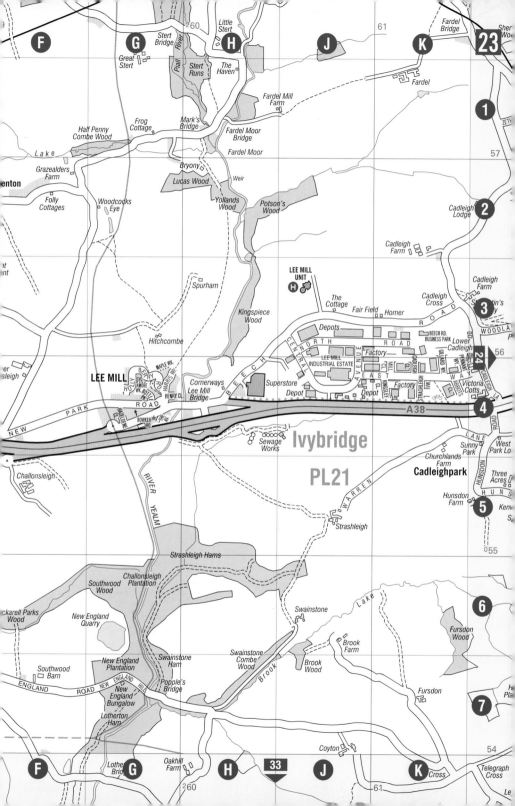

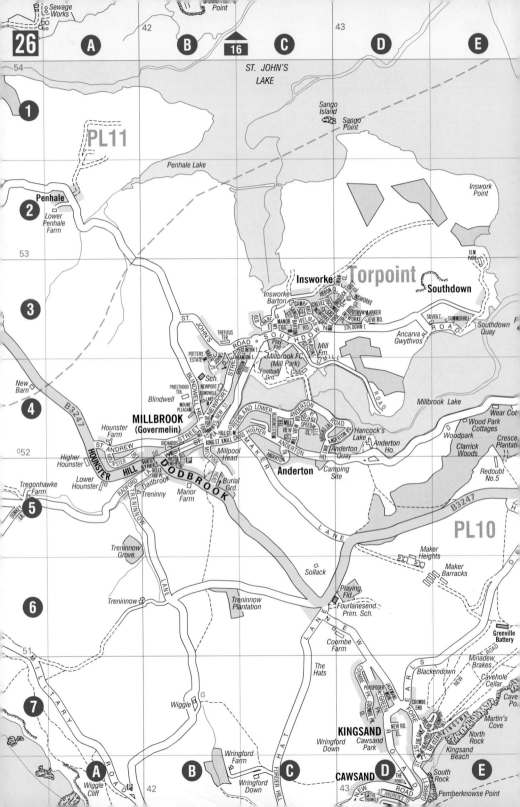

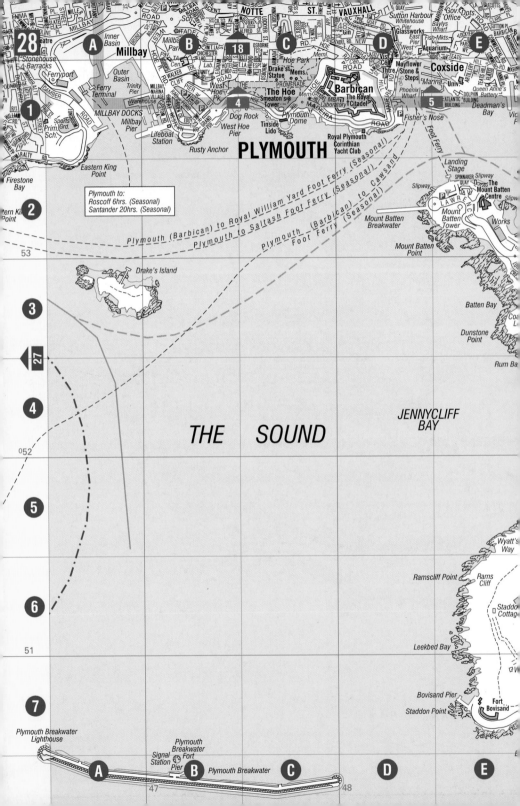

A Inner Basin
Millbay

B

18

C NOTTE ST.

D VAUXHALL

Sutton Harbour
Whitehouse
Glassworks
East
West
Pier
Fish-Mkts.

E Gov. Depts.
Office
Baylys
Wharf

Ferryport

Outer Basin
Trinity Pier

Ferry
Terminal

Millbay
Park

CHICHESTER

Hoe Park

Gin
RD.

Mayflower
Stone &
Steps

Aquarium

Coxside

Univ.

1 MILLBAY DOCKS
Millbay Pier

Warehouse

Millbay
Marina

West Hoe

Drake's
Statue
Mems.

Drake's
Dome

Smeaton's
Tower

Phoenix
Wharf

Fisher's
Nose

Marina

Atlantic
Building

Dolphin
Battery

Deadman's
Bay

Eastern King
Point

Sports
Grd.

Dog Rock

Tinside
Lido

Plymouth
Dome

Barbican
The Royal
Citadel

Queen Anne's

Firestone
Bay

Lifeboat
Station

West Hoe
Pier

Rusty Anchor

Royal Plymouth
Corinthian
Yacht Club

Landing
Stage

2 ern Ki
Point

PLYMOUTH

Plymouth to:
Roscoff 6hrs. (Seasonal)
Santander 20hrs. (Seasonal)

SPINNAKER
QUAY

Slipway

The
Mount Batten
Centre

Slipw

53

Plymouth (Barbican) to Royal William Yard Foot Ferry (Seasonal)

Plymouth to Saltash Foot Ferry (Seasonal)

Plymouth (Barbican) to Cawsand
Foot Ferry (Seasonal)

Mount Batten
Breakwater

Slipway

Mount
Batten
Tower

Works

Mount Batten
Point

3

Drake's Island

Batten Bay

Coa
L

Dunstone
Point

27

Rum Ba

4

THE   SOUND

JENNYCLIFF
BAY

052

5

Wyatt's
Way

Ramscliff Point

Rams
Cliff

6

Staddo
Cottag

51

Leekbed Bay

7

Bovisand Pier

Fort
Bovisand

Plymouth Breakwater
Lighthouse

Staddon Point

Plymouth
Breakwater
Fort
Pier

Signal
Station

A

B Plymouth Breakwater

C

D

E

47

48

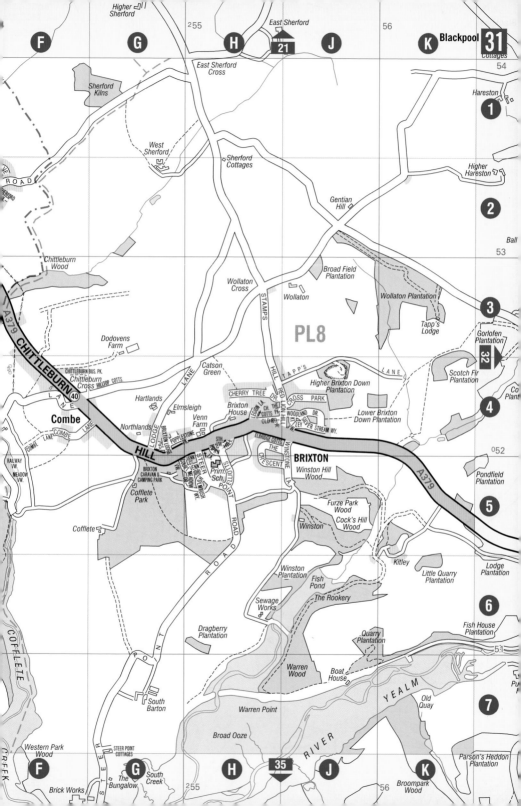

A   57   **B**   **C**   58   **D**   **E**

East Pitton
Farm

Warren
Wood

22

54

Hareston
Cottages

Hareston
Cross

1

Hareston

Lyneham Wood

Furzehill
Plantation

Furzehill

Furzehill
Cottage

Higher
Hareston

Efford
Farm

Lyneham
House

Treby
Farm

2

Lyneham
Cottage

Airstrip

53

Ball's Wood

Plymouth

PL8

Silverbridge

Wood
Cottage

Bedpark
Plantation

Allerco
Wo

3

Gorlofen

Jenny's Grove

Stonycross

Stonycross
Lodge

Tapp's
Lodge

31

Gorlofen
Plantation

Gorlofen
Lodge

Hall
Torrs

YEO PARK

Scotch Fir
Plantation

Colon
Plantation

Ewelis
Plantation

Cole Hill
Plantation

4

Yealmbri

Peasberry
Plantation

Mount
Pleasant

052

YEALMPTON

Eastern Torrs

Pondfield
Plantation

BOWDEN
FARM

HILL

YEALMBURY

ELM TREE

ELM TREE

Mill

Leat

5

A379

UNDERHAY

FORE ST.

MARKET ST.

NEW RD.

MILL LEAT CL.

MILIZAC
CL.

SPECULATION
COTTS.

SUNNYSIDE

CHURCH
PARK

CHURCH

Yealmpton
Prim. Sch.

YEALM

STRAY
PARK

MARJORY
WK.

Waltacre
Farm

TORR
BRIDGE

Black Torrs

PARK

WALK

Little Quarry
Plantation

Lodge
Plantation

Lodge

Rec.
Grd.

MARJORY
WK.

Sewage
Works

Rounds Nest

ROUNDSNEST

BOADVENTURE

FORD

RIVERSIDE

ORCHARD

CHAPEL RD.

TUCKERS CL.

PLOUGHMAN WY.

CREAMERY COOK CL.

ROCKDALE
CL.

Torr

6

Shipsen

Western
Torrs

WALTACRE

DIXON

TERRACE

THE ORCHARD

CRO...

CHURCH RD.

Rockdale

Higher Torr
Farm

Fish House
Plantation

51

Rough Torrs

Torr
Farm

Torr Ho.

The
Trees

Puslinch
Farm

Puslinch

Puslinch
Bridge

Rough Tor
Barn

Westpark

Two
Crosses

FORD ROAD

Cross Park
Ho.

Reservoir
(Covered)

Blowden
Wood

7

P

ASHCOMBE

Blowden
Farm

Heddon Wood

B3186

Seccombe
Wood

Parson's Heddon
Plantation

Ashcombe
Plantation

Gill's
Wood

HILL

Smutty Moo
Wood

A   57   **B**   Ashcombe   **C**   58   **D**   **E**

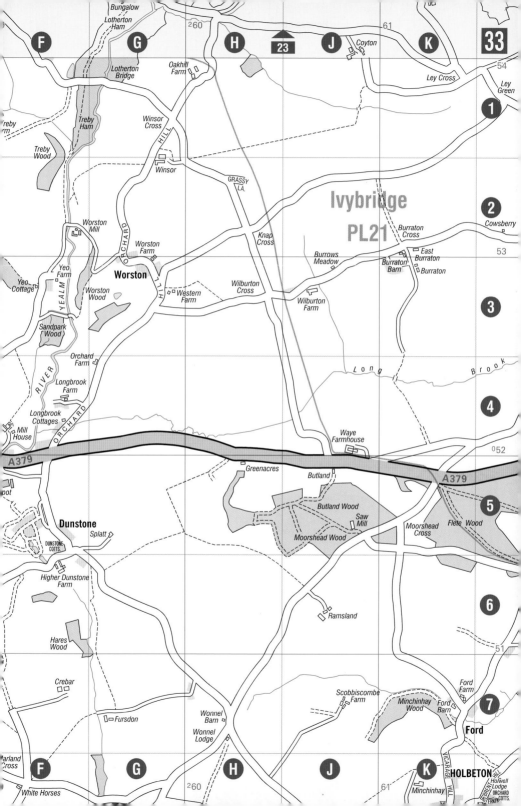

F · G · H · J · K

South Barton
255
Warren Point
Broad Ooze
31
Old Quay
56
Parson's Heddon Plantation

Western Park Wood
STEER POINT COTTAGES
The Bungalow
South Creek
Broompark Wood
Brusheshill Wood
Wrescombe

1

Brick Works
STEER POINT
Steer Point Plantation
M
Y
E
A
L
M
West Wood

050

COFFLETE CREEK
Steer Point Lodge
Steer Point

2

Boxcove Scout Camp
Wembury Wood
Hanaford Green

Crawl Wood

Reservoir (Covered)
B3186

3

PL8
Newton Downs
Kegwell
Richardson Dr.
Sewage Works
Livingstone Av.

49

Quay
South Wembury Court
Shortaflete Creek
Pump House
Butts Park Football & Cricket Grd.
Widey Cross
Lakeside Farm
Collaton Wood

4

Newton Wood
Pav.
BUTTS PK. COURT
The Butts

Plymouth
GUNSEY LANE
PARSONAGE ROAD
Parsonage Farm

Sewage Works
Membland Wood

5

Herons Reach
North Lodge
Beacon Hill House
Menryn Court Wood
The Lodge
Beacon Hill
Horsewells
Beech Cottages
THE PLEASAURE
ST CATHERINES
ARCH ST
Playing Field
Sch.
DILLS CL
THE GN
NEWTON FERRERS
THE FAIRWAY
ROAD
YEALM RD.
BRIDGEND
Newton Farm
Post Office Farm
Bridgend
Western Lodge
Hewster's Wood
Membland
PERCHES
CL.

48

MIDDLE LEIGH
BEACON HILL
COURT ROAD
WRIGHTS
Church Pk.
CH. R.
BISHOPS CT.
YEALM VW RD.
WIDEY HILL ROAD
Hoarstone
Hewster's Hill Wood

6

D
Y
E
A
L
M
RIVERSIDE ROAD
WEST
RIVERSIDE RD. EAST
Noss Creek
CREEK
Junket Corner
Great Prideaux

Ferry Wood
Fordhill Plantation
COMBE
PILLORY HILL
STOKE ROAD
NOSS MAYO
Pitts Hill Wood

N
E
W
T
O
N

Coombe Down
HILLSIDE COTTS.
HANNAFORD ROAD
SANDYWAY LA.
LAUNDRY
COACH H.
CREEKSIDE RD.
NEVELSTOKE RD.
MARSH
MIDDLECOMBE
Eastern Hill Wood
Rowden Farm

7

Brooking's Down Wood
Rowden

47

F · G · H · J · K

Little Worswell
HANNAFORD
255
Clevemoor
LANE
56
Stoke Cross
Revelstoke

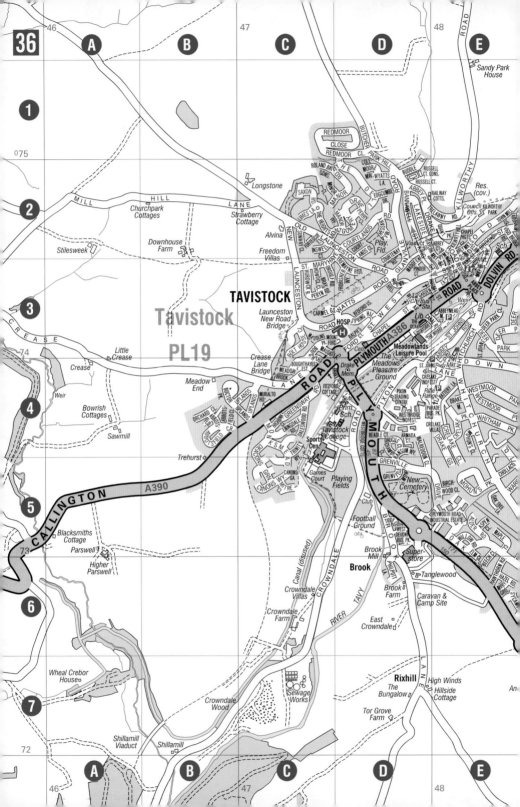

36

A   B   C   D   E

TAVISTOCK

Tavistock
PL19

Sandy Park House

REDMOOR CLOSE
REDMOOR CL.

Longstone

MILL HILL LANE

Churchpark Cottages
Strawberry Cottage
Stileweek
Downhouse Farm
Alvina
Freedom Villas

Launceston New Road Bridge
ROAD HOSP.
Crease Lane Bridge

CREASE
Little Crease
Crease
Weir
Bowrish Cottages
Sawmill
Trehurst

Meadow End
MURALTO HO.

Meadowlands Leisure Pool
The Meadows Pleasure Ground

PIXON TRADING CENTRE
WESTBRIDGE (INDEST)
CRELAKE VILLAS

Tavistock College
Sports Cen.
Games Court

Playing Fields

New Cemetery

CALLINGTON   A390

Blacksmiths Cottage
Parswell
Higher Parswell

Club

Football Ground

Brook Mill
Superstore
Tanglewood

Brook
Brook Farm

Crowndale Villas
Crowndale Farm

CROWNDALE
RIVER TAVY

East Crowndale

Caravan & Camp Site

Rixhill
High Winds
The Bungalow
Hillside Cottage

Wheal Crebor House

Crowndale Wood

Sewage Works

Tor Grove Farm

Shillamill Viaduct
Shillamill

A   B   C   D   E

37

Kennels
Kestrel
49

Nutley Farm

Exeter Lane Bri.
Boarding Houses
Kelly College
Playing Field
Weirs
Lower Rowden Wood

Kingford Farm

1

Mount House School
PARKWOOD ROAD
Games Court
Play. Fld.
Lower Rowden Wood
6 Pav. Sports Grd.
PARKWOOD
A386
WILMINGSTONE IND. EST.

075

PARKWOOD CT. YELVERTON
SUNSHINE TER.
Weir
Taviton Cotts.
Sunny Mount

2

TAVY ROAD
B3357
The Old Lodge
Taviton Mill House
Knoll Park
Redlands
Taviton

MOUNT
Ruswyn
Lodge Wood
Sluice
The Nook
Moorview

St. Peter's C of E Junior School
Play Fld.
Playgrd.
Torland Wood
Weir
Weir
Weir

3

GREENLANDS ESTATE
MILTON CHAUCER Road
Torfields
DARTMOOR NATIONAL PARK
74

Club House
DOWN ROAD
TAVISTOCK GOLF COURSE

4

Cricket Ground
WHITCHURCH DOWN
Res. (cov.)
TAVISTOCK GOLF COURSE
Pixie's Cross*

Trevaunance
Football Grd.
P

5

LAGOTT LANE
CLOSE
The Gate Cottage
Holwell
Caseytown
Venn Farm
73
Lower Venn
Venn

PRIORY
Whitchurch
The Chantry
Whitchurch House
Ckt. Grd.
The Lodge
Holwell Cottage
Middlemoor
Tarrywood

6
Whitchurch Primary School
Edgemoor Cottage
MOOR COTTAGES
The Barn
Birchey
Lower Statsford

Tiddy Brook
Shortsland
Higher Statsford
Bleak Ho.

CHURCH LANE
Budghill

ANDERTON
Anderton Cottage
Shorts Down

7
A386 ROAD
Higher Pennaton
Lower Pennaton
72

49
250
51

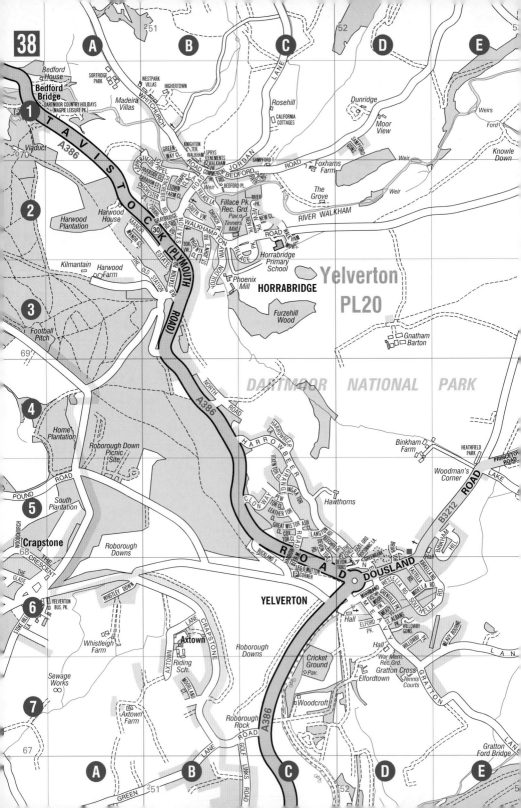

INDEX

Including Streets, Places & Areas, Hospitals etc., Industrial Estates,
Selected Flats & Walkways, Service Areas, Stations and Selected Places of Interest.

HOW TO USE THIS INDEX

1. Each street name is followed by its Postcode District, then by its Locality abbreviation(s) and then by its map reference;
e.g. **Abbotsbury Way** PL2: Plym . . . .7J **11** is in the PL2 Postcode District and the Plymouth Locality and is to be found in square 7J on page **11**. The page number is shown in bold type.

2. A strict alphabetical order is followed in which Av., Rd., St., etc. (though abbreviated) are read in full and as part of the street name;
e.g. **Broad La.** appears after **Broadlands Cl.** but before **Broadley Ct.**

3. Streets and a selection of flats and walkways that cannot be shown on the mapping, appear in the index with the thoroughfare to which they are connected shown in brackets; e.g. **Albion Ct.** PL11: Torp . . . .5E **16** (off Gravesend Gdns.)

4. Addresses that are in more than one part are referred to as not continuous.

5. Places and areas are shown in the index in BLUE TYPE and the map reference is to the actual map square in which the town centre or area is located and not to the place name shown on the map; e.g. ANDERTON 4C **26**

6. An example of a selected place of interest is Plympton Castle 4F **21**

7. An example of a station is Devonport Station (Rail) . . . .5J **17**, also included is Park & Ride.
e.g. Coypool (Park & Ride) 2B **20**

8. Service Areas are shown in the index in BOLD CAPITAL TYPE; e.g. **SALTASH SERVICE AREA** 2K **9**

9. An example of a Hospital, Hospice or selected Healthcare facility is DERRIFORD HOSPITAL 3G **13**

10. Map references for entries that appear on large scale pages **4** & **5** are shown first, with small scale map references shown in brackets;
e.g. **Abbey Pl.** PL1: Plym 5E **4** (7C **18**)

GENERAL ABBREVIATIONS

App. : Approach	**Dr.** : Drive	**La.** : Lane	**Rdbt.** : Roundabout
Arc. : Arcade	**E.** : East	**Lit.** : Little	**Shop.** : Shopping
Av. : Avenue	**Est.** : Estate	**Lwr.** : Lower	**Sth.** : South
Bri. : Bridge	**Fld.** : Field	**Mnr.** : Manor	**Sq.** : Square
Bldg. : Building	**Gdn.** : Garden	**Mkt.** : Market	**St.** : Street
Bldgs. : Buildings	**Gdns.** : Gardens	**Mdw.** : Meadow	**Ter.** : Terrace
Bungs. : Bungalows	**Ga.** : Gate	**Mdws.** : Meadows	**Trad.** : Trading
Bus. : Business	**Gt.** : Great	**M.** : Mews	**Up.** : Upper
Cen. : Centre	**Grn.** : Green	**Mt.** : Mount	**Va.** : Vale
Cir. : Circus	**Gro.** : Grove	**Mus.** : Museum	**Vw.** : View
Cl. : Close	**Hgts.** : Heights	**Nth.** : North	**Vs.** : Villas
Cnr. : Corner	**Ho.** : House	**Pde.** : Parade	**Vis.** : Visitors
Cotts. : Cottages	**Ind.** : Industrial	**Pk.** : Park	**Wlk.** : Walk
Ct. : Court	**Info.** : Information	**Pl.** : Place	**W.** : West
Cres. : Crescent	**Intl.** : International	**Ri.** : Rise	**Yd.** : Yard
Cft. : Croft	**Junc.** : Junction	**Rd.** : Road	

LOCALITY ABBREVIATIONS

Bere F : **Bere Ferrers**	Erm : **Ermington**	Mt Ed : **Mount Edgcumbe**	Tam F : **Tamerton Foliot**
Bitta : **Bittaford**	Fil : **Filham**	New F : **Newton Ferrers**	Tavi : **Tavistock**
Bovis : **Bovisand**	Harf : **Harford**	Noss M : **Noss Mayo**	Torp : **Torpoint**
Brixt : **Brixton**	Hatt : **Hatt**	N'ter : **Notter**	Torr : **Torr**
Buck M : **Buckland Monachorum**	Hem : **Hemerdon**	Plym : **Plymouth**	T'han : **Trehan**
C'eel : **Carkeel**	Holb : **Holbeton**	Plymp : **Plympton**	Trem : **Trematon**
Caws : **Cawsand**	Hooe : **Hooe**	Plyms : **Plymstock**	Trew : **Trewetha**
C'stone : **Crapstone**	Horr : **Horrabridge**	Rame : **Rame**	Wem : **Wembury**
Crem : **Cremyll**	Ivy : **Ivybridge**	Robo : **Roborough**	White : **Whitchurch**
Dev : **Devonport**	K'and : **Kingsand**	St E : **St Erney**	Wilc : **Wilcove**
Dous : **Dousland**	L'ake : **Landrake**	Salt : **Saltash**	Wors : **Worston**
Down T : **Down Thomas**	L Mill : **Lee Mill**	Smit : **Smithaleigh**	Yeal : **Yealmpton**
Drak : **Drakelands**	Mem : **Membland**	Spa : **Sparkwell**	Yelv : **Yelverton**
Dunst : **Dunstone**	Mill : **Millbrook**	Spri : **Spriddlestone**	
Elb : **Elburton**	Moor : **Moorhaven**	Stad : **Staddiscombe**	

A

Abbey Ct. PL1: Plym 5F **5**
PL19: Tavi 2E **36**
Abbeymead M. PL19: Tavi 3E **36**
Abbey Pl. PL1: Plym 5E **4** (7C **18**)
PL19: Tavi 2D **36**
(Bannawell St.)
PL19: Tavi 3E **36**
(Dolvin Rd.)
Abbey Ri. PL19: Tavi 3E **36**
Abbot Rd. PL21: Ivy 2B **24**
Abbotsbury Way PL2: Plym 7J **11**
Abbots Cl. PL21: L Mill 4K **23**
Abbots Ct. PL21: Ivy 3B **24**
Abbotsfield PL19: Tavi 4B **36**
Abbotsfield Cl. PL19: Tavi 4B **36**
Abbotsfield Cres. PL19: Tavi . . .4B **36**
Abbotts Rd. PL3: Plym 3D **18**

Aberdeen Av. PL5: Plym 5C **12**
Abingdon Rd.
PL4: Plym 1F **5** (5D **18**)
Abney Cres. PL6: Plym 1G **13**
Acklington Pl. PL5: Plym 3H **11**
Acland Rd. PL21: Ivy 2B **24**
Acorn Gdns. PL7: Plymp 2E **20**
Acre Cotts. PL1: Dev 5J **17**
Acre Pl. PL1: Dev 5J **17**
Activate Sports & Leisure 7F **13**
Adams Beck PL12: L'ake 2C **8**
Adams Cl. PL5: Plym 6H **11**
PL11: Torp 5B **16**
Adams Cres. PL11: Torp 5B **16**
Adam's La. PL9: Down T 2A **34**
Addison Rd. PL4: Plym . . .2F **5** (5D **18**)
Adelaide La.
PL1: Plym 5A **4** (7A **18**)
Adelaide Pl.
PL1: Plym 4A **4** (6A **18**)

Adelaide St.
PL1: Plym 4A **4** (6A **18**)
PL2: Plym 3J **17**
Adelaide St. Ope
PL1: Plym 4A **4** (6A **18**)
Adelaide Ter. PL1: Plym 2C **4**
Adit La. PL12: Salt 4B **10**
Admiral's Hard PL1: Dev 1K **27**
Admiralty Cotts.
PL1: Plym 2K **27**
Admiralty Rd. PL1: Dev 1K **27**
PL5: Plym 5F **11**
Admiralty St. PL1: Dev 1K **27**
PL2: Plym 2H **17**
Admiralty St. La. W.
PL1: Plym 1K **27**
Agaton Fort Rd. PL5: Plym 4J **11**
Agaton Rd. PL5: Plym 5H **11**
Ainslie Ter. PL2: Plym 1H **17**

Airborne Dr. PL6: Plym 3G **13**
(not continuous)
Aire Gdns. PL3: Plym 3H **19**
Alamein Ct. PL12: Salt 5A **10**
Alamein Rd. PL12: Salt 5A **10**
Albany St. PL1: Dev 6H **17**
Albemarle Vs. PL1: Plym 5J **17**
Albertha Cl. PL4: Plym . . .2G **5** (5E **18**)
Albert Rd. PL2: Dev 5H **17**
PL12: Salt 5C **10**
Albion Bungs. PL11: Torp 5E **16**
Albion Ct. PL11: Torp 5E **16**
(off Gravesend Gdns.)
Albion Dr. PL2: Plym 1A **18**
Albion Rd. PL11: Torp 5E **16**
Alcester Cl. PL2: Dev 4H **17**
Alcester St. PL2: Dev 4J **17**
Alden Wlk. PL6: Plym 1G **19**
Alderney Rd. PL6: Plym 7E **6**
Alder Rd. PL19: Tavi 5E **36**

Aldersley Wlk.—Benbow St.

Aldersley Wlk. PL6: Plym ... 7F 13
Alexandra Cl. PL9: Elb ... 1C 30
Alexandra Pl.
PL4: Plym ... 1G 5 (4D 18)
PL10: Mill ... 4B 26
(off Blindwell Hill)
Alexandra Rd. PL2: Plym ... 3J 17
PL4: Plym ... 1G 5 (4E 18)
PL6: Plym ... 5E 12
(off Morshead Rd.)
Alexandra Sq. PL12: Salt ... 5D 10
(off Fore St.)
Alexandra Ter. PL2: Plym ... 3J 17
Alfred Pl. PL2: Plym ... 3J 17
Alfred Rd. PL2: Plym ... 3J 17
Alfred St. PL1: Plym ... 6D 4 (7C 18)
Alger Wlk. PL6: Plym ... 1D 12
Alice La. PL1: Plym ... 4B 4
Alice St. PL1: Plym ... 4A 4 (6A 18)
Allenby Rd. PL2: Plym ... 2K 17
Allendale Rd.
PL4: Plym ... 1F 5 (5D 18)
Allens Rd. PL21: Ivy ... 2E 24
Allern La. PL5: Tam F ... 4C 6
Allerton Wlk. PL6: Plym ... 1G 19
Alleyn Gdns. PL3: Plym ... 7D 12
Allotment La. PL7: Plymp ... 5F 21
Alma Cotts.
PL4: Plym ... 5J 5 (7E 18)
Alma Rd. PL3: Plym ... 1B 4 (3A 18)
Alma St. PL4: Plym ... 5J 5 (7E 18)
Almeria Ct. PL7: Plymp ... 4E 20
Almond Dr. PL7: Plymp ... 2J 21
Alston Pk. PL7: Plymp ... 2E 20
Alton Pl. PL4: Plym ... 1G 5 (5D 18)
Alton Rd. PL4: Plym ... 1F 5 (5D 18)
Alvington St.
PL4: Plym ... 6K 5 (7F 19)
Alwin Pk. PL6: Plym ... 2F 13
Amacre Dr. PL9: Hooe ... 3G 29
Amados Cl. PL7: Plymp ... 4C 20
Amados Dr. PL7: Plymp ... 4D 20
Amados Ri. PL7: Plymp ... 4D 20
Amherst Rd.
PL3: Plym ... 1B 4 (5B 18)
Amherst Rd. La. East
PL3: Plym ... 1B 4 (4B 18)
Amity Pl. PL4: Plym ... 2G 5 (5D 18)
ANDERTON ... 4C 26
Anderton Cl. PL19: Whitc ... 7G 37
Anderton Ct. PL19: Whitc ... 7G 37
Anderton La. PL19: Whitc ... 7F 37
Anderton Ri. PL10: Mill ... 4C 26
Andurn Cl. PL9: Elb ... 3C 30
Ann's Pl. PL3: Plym ... 4K 17
Anson Ho. PL1: Plym ... 3B 4
Anson Pl. PL2: Dev ... 4J 17
PL4: Plym ... 4K 5 (6F 19)
Anstis St. PL1: Plym ... 3A 4 (6A 18)
Anthony Pk. PL19: Tavi ... 2F 37
(off Parkwood Rd.)
Antony ... 3A 16
Antony Gdns. PL2: Plym ... 7B 12
ANTONY PASSAGE ... 7K 9
Antony Rd. PL11: Torp ... 4D 16
Anzac Av. PL5: Plym ... 3K 11
Appleby Wlk. PL5: Plym ... 3C 12
Appledore Cl. PL6: Plym ... 1H 13
Appleton Tor Cl. PL3: Plym ... 2K 19
Apsley Ct.
PL4: Plym ... 1D 4 (5C 18)
Apsley Rd. PL4: Plym ... 1E 4 (5C 18)
Arbour, The PL6: Plym ... 2D 12
Arcadia PL9: Elb ... 3E 30
Arcadia Rd. PL9: Elb ... 3D 30
Archer Pl. PL1: Plym ... 2C 4 (5B 18)
Archers Ct. PL8: New F ... 4H 35
Archer Ter. PL1: Plym ... 3C 4 (6B 18)
Archotect Way PL5: Plym ... 7E 10
Archway Av. PL4: Plym ... 5G 19
Arden Gro. PL2: Plym ... 7B 12
Arimoor Gdns. PL19: Tavi ... 3G 37
Ark Royal Cl. PL5: Plym ... 7G 11
Arkwright Gdns. PL5: Plym ... 5J 11
Arley Cl. PL6: Plym ... 1G 13
Arlington Rd. PL4: Plym ... 4E 18
Armada Cen.
PL1: Plym ... 3D 4 (6C 18)
Armada Ct. PL19: Tavi ... 4D 36
Armada Memorial ... 7E 4 (1C 28)
Armada St. PL4: Plym ... 2F 5 (5D 18)
Armada Way
PL1: Plym ... 7D 4 (7C 18)
(not continuous)
Arnison Cl. PL9: Plyms ... 4K 29
Arnold's Point PL4: Plym ... 5H 19
Arnside Cl. PL6: Plym ... 4J 13
Arscott Gdns. PL9: Hooe ... 4H 29
Arscott La. PL9: Hooe ... 4H 29
Arthur Ter. PL11: Torp ... 6E 16
(off Bellevue Sq.)
Artillery Pl. PL4: Plym ... 7H 5 (1E 28)
Arun Cl. PL3: Plym ... 3H 19
Arundel Cres.
PL1: Plym ... 2B 4 (5B 18)
Arundel Ter. PL2: Dev ... 4J 17
(off Victoria Pl.)
Ashburgh Parc PL12: Salt ... 4J 9
Ashburnham Rd. PL5: Plym ... 4K 11
Ash Cl. PL20: Yelv ... 5C 38
Ashcombe Cl. PL7: Plymp ... 1D 20
Ashcombe Hill PL8: Yeal ... 7C 32
Ash Ct. PL21: Ivy, L Mill ... 3A 24
Ashdown Cl. PL6: Plym ... 4K 13
Ashdown Wlk. PL6: Plym ... 4K 13
Ashery Dr. PL9: Hooe ... 3H 29
Ashford Cl. PL3: Plym ... 4F 19
Ashford Cres. PL3: Plym ... 4F 19
Ashford Hill PL4: Plym ... 4F 19
Ashford Rd. PL4: Plym ... 4E 18
Ash Gro. PL2: Plym ... 1J 17
PL21: Ivy ... 3F 25
Ashleigh Cl. PL5: Tam F ... 7B 6
Ashleigh La. PL5: Tam F ... 4C 6
Ashleigh Way PL7: Plymp ... 4K 21
Ashley Pl. PL1: Plym ... 2B 4
Ashridge Gdns. PL5: Plym ... 5A 12
Ashton Cl. PL6: Plym ... 1H 13
Ashton M. PL12: Salt ... 4A 10
Ashton Way PL12: Salt ... 4A 10
Ashtree Cl. PL6: Plym ... 7J 7
Ashtree Gro. PL9: Elb ... 1D 30
Ashwood Cl. PL7: Plymp ... 3J 21
Ashwood Pk. Rd. PL7: Plymp ... 2K 21
Aspen Cl. PL19: Tavi ... 5E 36
Aspen Gdns. PL7: Plymp ... 3J 21
Astor Dr. PL4: Plym ... 5H 19
Athenaeum La.
PL1: Plym ... 5C 4 (7B 18)
Athenaeum Pl.
PL1: Plym ... 5D 4 (7C 18)
Athenaeum St.
PL1: Plym ... 6C 4 (7B 18)
Atherton Pl. PL2: Dev ... 4H 17
(off Charlotte St.)
Athlone Ho. PL1: Plym ... 5A 4
Atlantic Bldg.
PL4: Plym ... 7H 5 (1E 28)
Attwood M. PL3: Plym ... 4A 18
Auckland Rd. PL2: Plym ... 3K 17
Auctioneers Cl. PL7: Plymp ... 3E 20
Austin Av. PL2: Plym ... 2K 17
Austin Cres. PL6: Plym ... 6H 13
Avent Wlk. PL7: Plymp ... 1G 21
Avenue, The PL21: L Mill ... 4G 23
Avery Way PL12: Salt ... 2K 9
Avon Cl. PL3: Plym ... 2J 19
Avondale Ter. PL2: Plym ... 3H 17
Axe Cl. PL3: Plym ... 2J 19
AXTOWN ... 6B 38
Axtown La. PL20: Yelv ... 7B 38
Aycliffe Gdns. PL7: Plymp ... 5H 21
Aylesbury Cres. PL5: Plym ... 2A 12
Aylwin Cl. PL7: Plymp ... 2F 21
Ayreville Rd. PL2: Plym ... 1A 18
Azure Sth. PL1: Plym ... 7C 4

B

Babbacombe Cl. PL6: Plym ... 7K 13
Babis Farm Cl. PL12: Salt ... 6C 10
Babis Farm Ct. PL12: Salt ... 6C 10
Babis Farm M. PL12: Salt ... 5C 10
Babis Farm Row PL12: Salt ... 5C 10
Babis Farm Way PL12: Salt ... 6C 10
Babis La. PL12: Salt ... 6C 10
Back Hill PL12: Salt ... 5K 9
Back La. PL6: Robo ... 3F 7
PL7: Plymp ... 4F 21
Badgers Cl. PL21: Ivy ... 3B 24
Badgers Wlk. PL12: Salt ... 3A 10
Badger Vw. PL9: Plyms ... 4K 29
Bainbridge Av. PL3: Plym ... 1E 18
Bainbridge Ct. PL7: Plymp ... 1E 20
Bakers Cl. PL7: Plymp ... 3K 21
Bakers Pl. PL1: Dev ... 7J 17
Balfour Ter. PL2: Dev ... 4H 17
Ball Pk. PL12: Salt ... 6A 10
Balmoral Av. PL2: Plym ... 3J 17
Bampfylde Way PL6: Plym ... 1C 12
Bampton Rd. PL6: Plym ... 6K 13
Bannawell St. PL19: Tavi ... 2D 36
BARBICAN ... 7F 5 (1D 28)
Barbican, The PL1: Plym ... 6F 5
(New St.)
PL1: Plym ... 6G 5 (7D 18)
(White La.)
Barbican App.
PL4: Plym ... 6J 5 (7E 18)
Barbican Ct. PL4: Plym ... 6F 5
Barbican Glassworks ... 6G 5 (7D 18)
Barbican Leisure Pk. ... 6J 5 (7E 18)
Barbican Rd. PL7: Plymp ... 4F 21
Barbican Theatre ... 7G 5 (1D 28)
Barbury Cres. PL6: Plym ... 6G 7
Barcote Wlk. PL6: Plym ... 6H 13
Bardsey Cl. PL6: Plym ... 7F 7
Baring St. PL4: Plym ... 2H 5 (5E 18)
Barker's Hill PL12: Salt ... 5K 9
Barley Mkt. St. PL19: Tavi ... 2E 36
Barlow Gdns. PL2: Plym ... 1A 18
Barn Cl. PL7: Plymp ... 4A 22
PL21: Ivy ... 2B 24
Barndale Cres. PL6: Plym ... 1G 13
BARNE BARTON ... 7F 11
Barne Cl. PL5: Plym ... 7F 11
Barne La. PL5: Plym ... 6G 11
Barne Rd. PL5: Plym ... 7F 11
Barnfield Dr. PL7: Plymp ... 3K 21
Barnicott Cl. PL8: New F ... 5H 35
Barningham Gdns. PL6: Plym ... 1F 13
Barn Pk. PL12: Salt ... 4C 10
Barn Pk. Cotts. PL9: Plyms ... 1J 29
(off Millway Pl.)
Barn Pk. Rd. PL3: Plym ... 3C 18
Barnstaple Cl. PL6: Plym ... 7K 13
Barnwood Cl. PL9: Hooe ... 4K 29
Baron's Pyke PL21: Ivy ... 4F 25
Barossa Pl. PL11: Torp ... 6E 16
Barossa Rd. PL11: Torp ... 5E 16
Barrack Pl. PL1: Plym ... 7K 17
Barrack St. PL1: Dev ... 6H 17
Barrie Gdns. PL5: Plym ... 6D 12
Barrow Down PL12: Salt ... 4J 9
Bartholomew Rd. PL2: Plym ... 3K 17
Barton Av. PL2: Plym ... 3H 17
Barton Cl. PL7: Plymp ... 3K 21
PL9: Wem ... 3C 34
PL12: L'ake ... 1B 8
Barton M. PL10: Mill ... 3C 26
PL12: L'ake ... 2B 8
Barton Rd. PL9: Hooe ... 2G 29
Basinghall Cl. PL9: Plyms ... 5K 29
Basket Ope PL4: Plym ... 6F 5
Bath La. PL1: Plym ... 5B 4 (7B 18)
Bath Pl. PL1: Plym ... 5B 4
Bath Pl. W. PL1: Plym ... 5B 4
Bath St. PL1: Plym ... 6B 4 (7B 18)
Battershall Cl. PL9: Plyms ... 4A 30
Batter St. PL4: Plym ... 5F 5 (7D 18)
Battery La. PL19: Tavi ... 4E 36
Battery St. PL1: Plym ... 4A 4 (6A 18)
(not continuous)
Baydon Cl. PL6: Plym ... 6H 13
Bayly's Rd. PL9: Plyms ... 2G 29
Bayswater Rd.
PL1: Plym ... 2C 4 (5B 18)
Baytree Cl. PL6: Plym ... 1J 13
(off Elm Rd.)
Baytree Gdns. PL2: Plym ... 1K 17
Beach Vw. Cres. PL9: Wem ... 4B 34
Beacon Cl. PL21: Ivy ... 2D 24
Beacon Down Av. PL2: Plym ... 7A 12
Beaconfield Rd. PL2: Plym ... 2A 18
Beacon Hill PL8: New F ... 5F 35
BEACON PARK ... 1A 18
Beacon Pk. Rd. PL2: Plym ... 2K 17
Beacon Rd. PL21: Ivy ... 2D 24
Beacon Vw. PL21: Bitta ... 7K 25
Beadle Ct. PL19: Tavi ... 4D 36
Beagle Rd. PL1: Dev ... 7J 17
Beare Cl. PL9: Hooe ... 4G 29
Bearsdown Cl. PL6: Plym ... 7H 13
Bearsdown Rd. PL6: Plym ... 7H 13
Beatrice Av. PL2: Plym ... 3H 17
PL4: Plym ... 2J 5 (5E 18)
PL12: Salt ... 5B 10
Beatrice Gdns. PL12: Salt ... 5B 10
Beattie Rd. PL5: Plym ... 7E 10
Beatty Cl. PL6: Plym ... 3F 13
Beauchamp Cres. PL2: Plym ... 1B 18
Beauchamp Rd. PL2: Plym ... 1B 18
Beaudyn Wlk. PL6: Plym ... 1H 19
Beaufort Cl. PL5: Plym ... 7F 11
Beaufort Ho. PL4: Plym ... 5G 5
Beauly Cl. PL7: Plymp ... 3H 21
Beaumaris Gdns. PL3: Plym ... 7E 12
Beaumaris Rd. PL3: Plym ... 1E 18
Beaumont Av.
PL4: Plym ... 3G 5 (6D 18)
Beaumont Park ... 3H 5 (6E 18)
Beaumont Pl.
PL4: Plym ... 4G 5 (6D 18)
Beaumont Rd.
PL4: Plym ... 4G 5 (6E 18)
Beaumont St. PL2: Plym ... 3K 17
Beaumont Ter. PL12: Salt ... 3C 10
Beckford Cl. PL7: Plymp ... 3H 21
Beckham Pl. PL3: Plym ... 2F 19
Beckley Ct. PL1: Plym ... 3E 4 (6C 18)
Bede Gdns. PL5: Plym ... 6B 12
BEDFORD BRIDGE ... 1A 38
Bedford Gro. PL21: Ivy ... 3E 24
Bedford Pk. PL4: Plym ... 2G 5 (5D 18)
Bedford Pk. Vs.
PL4: Plym ... 1G 5 (5D 18)
Bedford Pl. PL19: Tavi ... 3E 36
(off Plymouth Rd.)
PL20: Horr ... 2B 38
Bedford Rd. PL9: Plyms ... 1K 29
PL20: Horr ... 2B 38
Bedford Sq. PL19: Tavi ... 3E 36
Bedford St. PL2: Plym ... 3J 17
Bedford Ter. PL4: Plym ... 2F 5 (5D 18)
Bedford Vs. PL19: Tavi ... 3D 36
Bedford Way
PL1: Plym ... 5E 4 (6C 18)
Beech Av. PL4: Plym ... 1F 29
Beech Cl. PL11: Torp ... 5D 16
PL19: Tavi ... 6E 36
Beech Ct. PL6: Plym ... 2J 13
Beechcroft Rd. PL2: Plym ... 1A 18
PL3: Plym ... 2F 19
Beeches, The PL20: Yelv ... 5D 38
Beechfield Av. PL20: Yelv ... 5C 38
Beechfield Gro. PL3: Plym ... 2D 18
Beech Rd. PL21: L Mill ... 4H 23
Beech Rd. Bus. Pk.
PL21: L Mill ... 3K 23
Beechwood Av.
PL4: Plym ... 1E 4 (4C 18)
Beechwood Ri. PL6: Plym ... 6K 13
Beechwood Ter. PL4: Plym ... 4C 18
Beechwood Way PL7: Plymp ... 3A 22
Beeston Wlk. PL3: Plym ... 1H 19
Belair Rd. PL2: Plym ... 1B 18
Belair Vs. PL2: Plym ... 1B 18
(off Montpelier Rd.)
Belgrave La. PL4: Plym ... 4D 18
Belgrave Rd. PL4: Plym ... 4D 18
Bellamy Cl. PL6: Plym ... 6F 13
Bell Cl. PL7: Plymp ... 1G 21
Belle Acre Cl. PL3: Plym ... 2E 18
Belle Vue PL11: Torp ... 5F 17
Belle Vue Av. PL9: Hooe ... 4G 29
Belle Vue Dr. PL9: Hooe ... 4G 29
Belle Vue Pl. PL10: Mill ... 5B 26
Belle Vue Ri. PL9: Hooe ... 4G 29
Belle Vue Rd. PL9: Hooe ... 4H 29
PL12: Salt ... 4C 10
Bellevue Sq. PL11: Torp ... 6E 16
Bellflower Cl. PL6: Robo ... 5H 7
Bellingham Cres. PL7: Plymp ... 4J 21
Belliver Ind. Est. PL6: Robo ... 5G 7
Belliver Way PL6: Robo ... 5G 7
Bell Pk. PL7: Plymp ... 1H 21
Belmont Pl. PL3: Plym ... 4K 17
Belmont Rd. PL21: Ivy ... 4D 24
Belmont St. PL1: Plym ... 4B 4 (6B 18)
Belmont Vs. PL3: Plym ... 5K 17
Belstone Cl. PL5: Plym ... 4K 11
Belvedere Rd. PL4: Plym ... 6G 19
Benbow St. PL2: Dev ... 4J 17

40 A-Z Plymouth

College Av. PL4: Plym 3D **18**
PL19: Tavi 2F **37**
College Dean Cl. PL6: Plym 2H **13**
College La. PL4: Plym 4D **18**
College Pk. Pl. PL3: Plym 3D **18**
College Rd. PL2: Plym 3H **17**
College Vw. PL3: Plym 4D **18**
Colliers Cl. PL9: Wem 3C **34**
Collin Cl. PL5: Plym 6G **11**
Collingwood Av. PL4: Plym 7F **19**
Collingwood Rd. PL1: Plym 5K **17**
Collingwood Vs. *PL1: Plym 5K **17***
(off Collingwood Rd.)
Colne Gdns. PL3: Plym 3G **19**
Colston Cl. PL6: Plym 1G **13**
Coltishall Cl. PL5: Plym 3J **11**
Coltness Rd. PL9: Elb 4C **30**
Coltsfield Cl. PL6: Plym 7G **13**
Columbus Cl. PL5: Plym 5F **11**
Colwill Rd. PL6: Plym 4K **13**
Colwill Wlk. PL6: Plym 4A **14**
Colwyn Rd. PL11: Torp 5D **16**
COMBE 4F **31**
Combe Down La.
PL8: Noss M 6G **35**
Combe La. PL8: Brixt 4F **31**
Combined Court Cen.
Plymouth 5E **4** (7C **18**)
Combley Dr. PL6: Plym 3J **13**
Commercial Ope PL4: Plym 6J **5**
Commercial Pl. PL4: Plym 7J **5**
Commercial Rd.
PL4: Plym 6J **5** (7E **18**)
PL20: Horr 2B **38**
Commercial St.
PL4: Plym 6J **5** (7E **18**)
Common La. PL6: Robo 1E **6**
Compass Dr. PL7: Plymp 1H **21**
Compton Av. PL3: Plym 3E **18**
Compton Knoll Cl. PL3: Plym . . .2F **19**
Compton Leigh PL3: Plym 2F **19**
Compton Pk. Rd. PL3: Plym 3E **18**
Compton Va. PL3: Plym 3F **19**
Congreve Gdns. PL5: Plym 6B **12**
Coniston Gdns. PL6: Plym 3E **12**
Connaught Av. PL4: Plym 4D **18**
Connaught La. PL4: Plym 4D **18**
Conqueror Dr. PL5: Plym 6D **12**
Conrad Rd. PL5: Plym 6B **12**
Consort Cl. PL3: Plym 1D **18**
Constable Cl. *PL5: Plym 5C **12***
(off Cowley Rd.)
Constance Pl.
PL1: Plym 3A **4** (6A **18**)
Constantine St.
PL4: Plym 4G **5** (6D **18**)
Convent Cl. PL12: Salt 4B **10**
Conway Gdns. PL2: Plym 1A **18**
Conyngham Ct. PL6: Plym 7F **13**
Cooban Ct. PL6: Plym 7F **13**
Cook Ct. PL12: Salt 4J **9**
Cookworthy Rd. PL2: Plym 2J **17**
Coombe Dean Sports Cen. 3B **30**
Coombe End PL10: K'and 7D **26**
Coombe La. PL5: Tam F 1B **12**
Coombe Pk. PL10: Caws 7D **26**
PL12: Salt 5C **10**
Coombe Pk. Cl. PL10: Caws 7D **26**
Coombe Pk. La. PL5: Plym 4K **11**
Coombe Pk. La. Sth.
PL5: Plym 4K **11**
Coombe Rd. PL12: Salt 6C **10**
Coombe Vw. *PL2: Plym 1H **17***
(off Ainslie Ter.)
Coombe Way PL5: Plym 6J **11**
Copleston Rd. PL6: Plym 2C **12**
Coppard Mdws. PL7: Plymp 2C **20**
Copper Beech Way PL6: Plym 7H **7**
Copperfields PL20: Horr 2A **38**
Coppers Pk. PL6: Plym 7K **7**
Coppice, The PL21: Ivy 4B **24**
Coppice Gdns. PL5: Plym 5D **12**
Coppice Wood Dr. PL6: Plym 6H **7**
Copse Cl. PL7: Plymp 4E **20**
Copse Rd. PL7: Plymp 4E **20**
Copthorne Gdns. PL9: Plyms 4A **30**
Corea Ter. PL1: Dev 6K **17**
Corfe Av. PL3: Plym 1E **18**
Corfe Cl. PL21: Ivy 4E **24**
Coringdean Cl. PL6: Plym 1G **13**
Corner Brake PL6: Plym 7J **7**
Cornfield Gdns. PL7: Plymp 1J **21**
Cornwall Beach PL1: Dev 6G **17**
Cornwall St. PL1: Dev 6G **17**
PL1: Plym 4C **4** (6B **18**)
(not continuous)
Cornwall St. Flats *PL1: Dev 6G **17***
(off Cornwall St.)
Cornwood Rd. PL7: Plymp 4J **21**
PL21: Ivy 3B **24**
Cornworthy Cl. PL2: Plym 1K **17**
Coronation Cotts. PL11: Torp 5E **16**
Coronation Pl. PL5: Plym 7H **11**
Corondale Rd. PL2: Plym 1A **18**
Corporation Rd. PL2: Plym 1C **18**
Corsham Cl. PL6: Plym 1G **13**
Cory Ct. PL9: Wem 2D **34**
Cosdon Pl. PL6: Plym 6E **12**
Costly St. PL21: Ivy 3E **24**
Cotehele Av. PL2: Plym 3J **17**
PL4: Plym 5K **5** (7F **19**)
Cot Hill PL7: Plymp 3C **20**
Cot Hill Cl. PL7: Plymp 2B **20**
Cot Hill Dr. PL7: Plymp 3C **20**
Cot Hill Trad. Est. PL7: Plymp . . .2B **20**
Cottage M. PL7: Plymp 4F **21**
Cotton Cl. PL7: Plymp 4G **21**
County Cl. PL7: Plymp 3H **21**
Court, The PL6: Plym 7H **7**
PL12: Salt 5K **9**
Courtenay Rd. PL19: Tavi 2D **36**
Courtenay St.
PL1: Plym 5D **4** (6C **18**)
Courtfield Rd. PL3: Plym 3E **18**
Courtland Cres. PL7: Plymp 1E **20**
Courtlands PL12: Salt 6B **10**
Courtlands Cl. PL19: Tavi 2D **36**
Courtlands Rd. PL19: Tavi 2D **36**
Court Rd. PL8: New F 5E **34**
(not continuous)
Court Vw. PL8: Brixt 5G **31**
Court Wood PL8: New F 4F **35**
Cove Mdw. PL11: Wilc 2D **16**
Coverdale Pl. PL5: Plym 6A **12**
Cowdray Cl. PL12: Salt 5B **10**
Cowdray Ter. PL12: Salt 6B **10**
Cowley Rd. PL5: Plym 4C **12**
Cox's Cl. PL6: Plym 6G **13**
COXSIDE 6J **5** (1E **28**)
Cox Tor Cl. PL20: Yelv 5C **38**
Cox Tor Rd. PL19: Tavi 3G **37**
Coypool (Park & Ride) 2B **20**
Coypool Rd. PL7: Plymp 2B **20**
CRABTREE 3J **19**
Crabtree Cl. PL3: Plym 3A **20**
Crabtree Vs. PL3: Plym 3K **19**
Crackston Cl. PL6: Plym 1G **19**
Craigie Dr. PL1: Plym 3A **4** (6A **18**)
Craigmore Av. PL2: Plym 3J **17**
Cramber Cl. PL6: Robo 5H **7**
PL19: Tavi 4D **36**
Cranbourne Av.
PL4: Plym 2K **5** (5F **19**)
Cranfield PL7: Plymp 1D **20**
Cranmere Rd. PL3: Plym 2F **19**
Crantock Ter. PL2: Plym 3K **17**
CRAPSTONE 6A **38**
Crapstone Rd. PL20: Yelv 6B **38**
Crashaw Cl. PL5: Plym 4C **12**
Craven Av. PL4: Plym 2K **5** (5F **19**)
Crawford Rd.
PL1: Plym 1A **4** (5A **18**)
Creamery Cl. PL8: Torr 6D **32**
Crease La. PL19: Tavi 3A **36**
Crediton Wlk. PL6: Plym 7K **13**
Creedy Rd. PL3: Plym 3H **19**
Creekside Rd. PL8: Noss M 6G **35**
Crelake Cl. PL19: Tavi 4E **36**
Crelake Ind. Est. PL19: Tavi 4D **36**
Crelake Pk. PL19: Tavi 4E **36**
Crelake Vs. PL19: Tavi 4E **36**
CREMYLL 2H **27**
Cremyll Rd. PL11: Torp 6E **16**
Cremyll St. PL1: Plym 7K **17**
Crescent, The
PL1: Plym 5C **4** (7B **18**)
PL8: Brixt 4H **31**
PL12: L'ake 1C **8**
PL20: C'stone 6A **38**
Crescent Av.
PL1: Plym 6C **4** (7B **18**)
Crescent Av. M. PL1: Plym 6C **4**
Crescent Gdns. PL21: Ivy 2D **24**
Crescent Rd. PL21: Ivy 2D **24**
Cressbrook Cl. PL6: Plym 5A **14**
Cressbrook Dr. PL6: Plym 5A **14**
Cressbrook Wlk. PL6: Plym 5K **13**
Crestfield Ri. PL21: Ivy 3C **24**
Cresthill Rd. PL2: Plym 1A **18**
Crofters Ct. PL21: Fil 4G **25**
Croft Pk. *PL6: Plym 7H **7***
(off Copper Beech Way)
Cromartie Rd. *PL4: Plym 7G **19***
(off Cavendish Rd.)
Cromer Cl. PL6: Plym 7F **7**
Cromer Wlk. PL6: Plym 7F **7**
Cromwell Ga. PL6: Plym 7H **7**
Cromwell Rd.
PL4: Plym 5K **5** (7F **19**)
Crookeder Cl. PL9: Plyms 4B **30**
Cross Hill PL2: Dev 4H **17**
Cross Pk. PL8: Brixt 4J **31**
Cross Pk. Av. PL6: Plym 6E **12**
Cross Pk. Rd. PL6: Plym 6E **12**
PL9: Wem 3B **34**
Cross Pk. Way PL6: Plym 6E **12**
Crossway PL7: Plymp 1D **20**
Crossway Av. PL4: Plym 5G **19**
Crossways PL9: Wem 3B **34**
Crowndale Av. PL3: Plym 2F **19**
Crowndale Rd. PL19: Tavi 6C **36**
Crown Gdns. PL6: Plym 6F **13**
CROWNHILL 6F **13**
Crownhill Fort 4E **12**
Crownhill Fort Rd. PL6: Plym . . .4E **12**
Crownhill Rd. PL5: Plym 4J **11**
PL6: Plym 4A **12**
Crow Pk. PL3: Plym 3E **18**
Croydon Gdns. PL5: Plym 3H **11**
Crozier Rd. PL4: Plym 4E **18**
Crylla Valley Cotts.
PL12: N'ter 1D **8**
Cuffe Rd. PL3: Plym 4A **18**
Culbin Grn. PL6: Plym 7J **13**
Culdrose Cl. PL5: Plym 4H **11**
Culme Rd. PL3: Plym 3F **19**
Culver Cl. PL6: Plym 7F **13**
Culver Ct. *PL12: Salt 5C **10***
(off Culver Rd.)
Culver Rd. PL12: Salt 5C **10**
Culver Way PL6: Plym 7E **12**
Culverwood Cl. PL7: Plymp 2K **21**
CUMBERLAND CENTRE 7J **17**
Cumberland Rd. PL1: Dev 7J **17**
Cumberland St. PL1: Dev 6H **17**
Cumble Tor La. PL12: Trem 4E **8**
Cundy Cl. PL7: Plymp 1B **20**
Cunliffe Av. PL9: Hooe 3F **29**
Cunningham Rd. PL5: Tam F 6B **6**
Cunningham Way *PL12: Salt 4A **10***
(off Callington Rd.)
Curlew M. PL3: Plym 4H **19**
Cursons Way PL21: Ivy 3B **24**
Curtis St. PL1: Dev 7H **17**
Custom Ho. La.
PL1: Plym 7B **4** (1B **28**)
Cypress Cl. PL7: Plymp 3K **21**

D

Dairy La. PL1: Plym 2A **4** (5A **18**)
PL21: Ivy 3E **24**
Dale Av. PL6: Plym 1H **19**
Dale Gdns. PL4: Plym 1E **4** (4C **18**)
Dale Rd. PL4: Plym 1D **4** (4C **18**)
Daleswood Rd. PL19: Tavi 4C **36**
Dalton Gdns. PL5: Plym 4H **11**
Damerel Cl. PL1: Dev 6J **17**
Danum Dr. PL7: Plymp 5J **21**
Darklake Cl. PL6: Plym 2K **13**
Darklake La. PL6: Plym 6J **7**
Darklake Vw. PL6: Plym 2J **13**
Dark St. La. PL7: Plymp 3F **21**
Dart Cl. PL3: Plym 2J **19**
Dartington Wlk. PL6: Plym 7K **13**
Dartmeet Av. PL3: Plym 2G **19**
Dartmoor Country Holidays
PL20: Horr 1A **38**
Dartmoor National Pk.
. . . . .4H **37**, 4C **38** & 1G **25**
Dartmoor Vw. PL4: Plym 5H **19**
PL12: Salt 3B **10**
Dartmouth Wlk. PL6: Plym 7K **13**
(not continuous)
Darton Cotts. *PL12: Salt 4K **9***
(off Thorn La.)
Darwin Cres. PL3: Plym 3J **19**
Dathan Cl. PL19: Tavi 3E **36**
Daucus Cl. PL19: Tavi 4D **36**
Davenham Cl. PL6: Plym 1G **13**
David Cl. PL7: Plymp 2G **21**
Davids La. PL21: Fil 3H **25**
David Southgate Ct. PL1: Plym . . .5A **4**
Davy Cl. PL11: Torp 5C **16**
Davy Rd. PL6: Plym 3H **13**
Dawes La. PL9: Elb 2E **30**
PL10: Mill 4B **26**
Dawlish Wlk. PL6: Plym 1K **19**
Daws Ct. PL12: Salt 5D **10**
Dawson Cl. PL5: Plym 6H **11**
Daymond Rd. PL5: Plym 5G **11**
Dayton Cl. PL6: Plym 5D **12**
Deacon Cl. PL12: Salt 6C **10**
Deacon Dr. PL12: Salt 6C **10**
Deacons Grn. PL19: Tavi 4C **36**
Dean Cross PL9: Plyms 2K **29**
Dean Cross Rd. PL9: Plyms 2K **29**
Dean Hill PL9: Plyms 2K **29**
Dean Pk. Rd. PL9: Plyms 2J **29**
Dean Rd. PL7: Plymp 2E **20**
Debden Cl. PL5: Plym 3G **11**
Deeble Cl. PL7: Plymp 1F **21**
Deep La. PL7: Plymp 6K **21**
Deer Leap PL19: Tavi 4F **37**
Deer Pk. PL12: Salt 4C **10**
PL21: Ivy 3F **25**
Deer Pk. Cl. PL19: Tavi 3E **36**
Deer Pk. Cres. PL19: Tavi 3E **36**
Deer Pk. Dr. PL3: Plym 1H **19**
Deer Pk. La. PL19: Tavi 3E **36**
Deer Pk. Rd. PL19: Tavi 3E **36**
Defoe Cl. PL5: Plym 5B **12**
Delacombe Cl. PL7: Plymp 1G **21**
De-la-Hay Av.
PL3: Plym 1A **4** (5A **18**)
Delamere Rd. PL6: Plym 1H **19**
Delamore Cl. PL21: Ivy 3B **24**
Delaware Gdns. PL2: Plym 1J **17**
Delgany Dr. PL6: Plym 2F **13**
Delgany Vw. PL6: Plym 2F **13**
Delgany Vs. PL6: Plym 2F **13**
Dell, The PL7: Plymp 2C **20**
PL19: Tavi 2D **36**
Dellohay Pk. PL12: Salt 3A **10**
Dengie Cl. PL7: Plymp 3J **21**
Denham Cl. PL5: Plym 5B **12**
Dennis Cl. PL5: Plym 1F **17**
Deptford Pl. PL4: Plym . . .2G **5** (5D **18**)
Derby Rd. PL5: Plym 3B **12**
DERRIFORD 3G **13**
Derriford Bus. Pk. PL6: Plym 4F **13**
Derriford Health & Leisure Cen.
. . . . .4H **13**
DERRIFORD HOSPITAL 3G **13**
Derriford Pk. PL6: Plym 4F **13**
Derriford Rd. PL6: Plym 3F **13**
Derry Av. PL4: Plym 1E **4** (5C **18**)
Derry's Cross
PL1: Plym 5C **4** (7B **18**)
Derwent Av. PL3: Plym 3H **19**
Desborough La.
PL4: Plym 4K **5** (6F **19**)
Desborough Rd.
PL4: Plym 4J **5** (6E **18**)
Deveron Cl. PL7: Plymp 3H **21**
Devon Enterprise Facility
PL6: Robo 4G **7**
Devonia Cl. PL7: Plymp 1F **21**
DEVONPORT 5J **17**
Devonport Column 7H **17**
Devonport Hill PL1: Dev 7J **17**
PL10: K'and 7E **26**
Devonport Pk. 5H **17**
Devonport Pk. PL1: Dev 6J **17**
Devonport Playhouse *6H **17***
(off Fore St.)
Devonport Rd. PL1: Plym 6J **17**
PL3: Plym 4K **17**
Devonport Station (Rail) 5J **17**
Devonshire Ct. PL11: Torp 5E **16**
Devonshire Health & Raquets Club
. . . . .3G **13**
Devonshire Ho. PL1: Plym 5B **4**

Devonshire Mdws.—Fegen Rd.

Devonshire Mdws. PL6: Robo ... 4G 7
Devonshire St. PL4: Plym ... 3G 5
Devon Ter. PL3: Plym ... 4D 18
Devon Tors PL20: Yelv ... 6D 38
Devon Tors Rd. PL20: Yelv ... 5C 38
Dewar Wlk. PL5: Plym ... 5J 11
Diamond Av.
PL4: Plym ... 2H 5 (5E 18)
Dickens Rd. PL5: Plym ... 5A 12
Dickiemoor La. PL5: Plym ... 5B 12
Dieppe Cl. *PL1: Dev ... 6J 17*
(off St Nazaire App.)
Digby Gro. PL5: Plym ... 2J 11
Dillons PL8: New F ... 5H 35
Dingle Rd. PL2: Plym ... 2K 17
PL7: Plymp ... 2D 20
Dingwall Av. PL5: Plym ... 4D 12
Dinnaton Golf Course ... 1B 24
Dipper Dr. PL19: Whitc ... 6F 37
Dirty La. PL12: C'eel ... 2H 9
Discovery Hgts. PL1: Plym ... 3E 4
Discovery Rd. PL1: Dev ... 7J 17
Discovery Wharf *PL4: Plym ... 5G 5*
(off North Quay)
Distine Cl. PL3: Plym ... 1G 19
Dittisham Wlk. PL6: Plym ... 7K 13
Ditton Ct. PL6: Plym ... 7F 13
Dixon Pl. PL2: Dev ... 4J 17
Dixon Ter. PL8: Torr ... 6C 32
Dockray Cl. PL6: Plym ... 3J 13
Dockyard Station (Rail) ... 4H 17
Doctors Steps *PL8: New F ... 6F 35*
(off Yealm Rd.)
Dodbrook PL10: Mill ... 5B 26
Doddridge Cl. PL9: Plyms ... 5A 30
Doidges Farm Cl. PL6: Plym ... 7G 13
Dolphin Bldg.
PL4: Plym ... 7H 5 (1E 28)
Dolphin Cl. PL9: Plyms ... 3A 30
Dolphin Ct. PL11: Torp ... 5A 16
Dolphin Ct. Rd. PL9: Plyms ... 3A 30
Dolphin Ho. PL4: Plym ... 5G 5
Dolphin Sq. PL9: Plyms ... 2A 30
Dolvin Rd. PL19: Tavi ... 3E 36
Donkey La. PL10: Mill ... 5A 26
PL21: Ivy ... 3D 24
Donnington Dr. PL3: Plym ... 1G 19
Dorchester Av. PL5: Plym ... 3C 12
Doreena Rd. PL9: Elb ... 2D 30
Dormy Av. PL3: Plym ... 3E 18
Dorsmouth Ter. PL7: Plymp ... 4F 21
Douglas Dr. PL9: Plyms ... 3B 30
Douglass Rd. PL3: Plym ... 2H 19
Douro Ct. PL21: Ivy ... 3E 24
Dousland Rd.
PL20: Dous, Yelv ... 6D 38
Dovedale Rd. PL2: Plym ... 1K 17
Dove Gdns. PL3: Plym ... 2J 19
Dover Rd. PL6: Plym ... 4K 13
Down Cl. PL12: Salt ... 6K 9
Downfield Dr. PL7: Plymp ... 3G 21
Downfield Wlk. PL7: Plymp ... 3G 21
Downfield Way PL7: Plymp ... 3G 21
Downgate Gdns. PL2: Plym ... 7C 12
Downham Gdns. PL5: Tam F ... 7B 6
Downhorne Pk. PL9: Plyms ... 3A 30
Downlea PL19: Tavi ... 4F 37
Down Pk. Dr. PL19: Tavi ... 4F 37
Down Rd. PL7: Plymp ... 3K 21
PL19: Tavi ... 4E 36
Downside Av. PL6: Plym ... 1H 19
DOWN THOMAS ... 7H 29
Downton Cl. PL1: Plym ... 2A 4 (5A 18)
Drake Cir. PL1: Plym ... 4F 5 (6C 18)
PL4: Plym ... 3F 5 (6D 18)
Drake Ct. PL4: Plym ... 3J 5 (6E 18)
PL5: Plym ... 3H 11
Drakefield Dr. PL12: Salt ... 4D 10
Drake Gdns. PL19: Tavi ... 4E 36
Drake Rd. PL19: Tavi ... 2D 36
Drakes Cl. PL6: Plym ... 2E 12
Drake's Statue ... 7D 4 (1C 28)
Drake Vs. PL19: Tavi ... 4D 36
Drake Way PL9: Plyms ... 2K 29
Drax Gdns. PL6: Plym ... 7D 12
Drayton Rd. PL5: Plym ... 6B 12
Drina La. PL5: Plym ... 5H 11
Drive, The PL3: Plym ... 1D 18
Drovers Way PL21: Ivy ... 2B 24
Drummond Cl. PL2: Plym ... 1J 17
Drummond Pl. PL1: Dev ... 5J 17
Drunken Bri. Hill PL7: Plymp ... 5D 20
Dryburgh Cres. PL2: Plym ... 1K 17
Dryden Av. PL5: Plym ... 6B 12
Ducane Wlk. PL6: Plym ... 6G 13
Duck La. PL12: Trem ... 3F 9
Duckworth St. PL2: Dev ... 4K 17
Ducky La. PL12: L'ake ... 1C 8
Dudley Gdns. PL6: Plym ... 7G 13
Dudley Rd. PL7: Plymp ... 3C 20
Dukes Ryde, The PL9: Plyms ... 2A 30
Duke St. PL1: Dev ... 6H 17
PL19: Tavi ... 3E 36
Duloe Gdns. PL2: Plym ... 7B 12
Dumfries Av. PL5: Plym ... 4C 12
Duncan St. PL1: Dev ... 7H 17
Dunclair Pk. PL3: Plym ... 3J 19
Duncombe Av. PL5: Plym ... 4J 11
Dundas St. PL2: Dev ... 4K 17
Dundonald St. PL2: Dev ... 4J 17
Dunheved Rd. PL12: Salt ... 5C 10
Dunkeswell Cl. PL2: Plym ... 7J 11
Dunley Wlk. PL6: Plym ... 6H 13
Dunnet Rd. PL6: Plym ... 1C 12
Dunraven Dr. PL6: Plym ... 2E 12
Dunster Cl. PL7: Plymp ... 4K 21
Dunsterville Rd. PL21: Ivy ... 2F 25
DUNSTONE ... 5F 33
Dunstone Av. PL9: Plyms ... 2B 30
Dunstone Cl. PL9: Plyms ... 2A 30
Dunstone Cotts. PL8: Dunst ... 5F 33
Dunstone Dr. PL9: Plyms ... 2A 30
Dunstone La. PL9: Elb ... 2C 30
Dunstone Rd. PL5: Plym ... 4J 11
PL9: Plyms ... 2A 30
Dunstone Vw. PL9: Elb, Plyms ... 2B 30
Durban Rd. PL3: Plym ... 3G 19
Durham Av. PL4: Plym ... 2K 5 (5F 19)
Durham Cotts. PL1: Plym ... 2B 4
Durnford St. PL1: Plym ... 7K 17
Durnford St. Ope PL1: Plym ... 7K 17
Durrant Cl. PL1: Dev ... 5H 17
Durris Cl. PL6: Plym ... 3J 13
Durris Gdns. PL6: Plym ... 3J 13
Durwent Cl. PL9: Hooe ... 3F 29
Duxford Cl. PL5: Plym ... 2H 11
Dymond Ct. PL12: Salt ... 5C 10
Dynevor Cl. PL3: Plym ... 1E 18

E

Eagle Cl. PL7: Plymp ... 4K 21
Eagle Rd. PL7: Plymp ... 3K 21
Earl's Acre PL3: Plym ... 1B 4 (4B 18)
Earls Dr. PL10: K'and, Mill ... 7D 26
Earls Mill Rd. PL7: Plymp ... 2F 21
Earls Wood Cl. PL6: Plym ... 4A 14
Earls Wood Dr. PL6: Plym ... 4A 14
Eastbury Av. PL5: Plym ... 5K 11
Eastcote Cl. PL6: Plym ... 1G 13
Eastella Rd. PL20: Yelv ... 6D 38
East End PL9: Plyms ... 1H 29
Easterdown Cl. PL9: Plyms ... 2A 30
Easterntown PL8: Holb ... 7K 33
Eastern Wood Rd.
PL7: Plymp ... 3A 22
Eastfield Av. PL9: Hooe ... 3H 29
Eastfield Cres. PL3: Plym ... 1F 19
Eastlake Ope
PL1: Plym ... 4F 5 (6D 18)
Eastlake St. PL1: Plym ... 3E 4 (6C 18)
East Pk. Av. PL4: Plym ... 1E 4 (5C 18)
East St. PL1: Plym ... 5A 4 (7A 18)
(not continuous)
East Vw. *PL3: Plym ... 4K 17*
(off Ann's Pl.)
East Way PL21: L Mill ... 4J 23
Ebrington St.
PL4: Plym ... 4G 5 (6D 18)
Echo Cres. PL5: Plym ... 5C 12
Eddystone Cl. PL3: Plym ... 2H 19
Eddystone Ter. PL1: Plym ... 1B 28
Eddy Thomas Wlk. PL5: Plym ... 3B 12
Eden Cotts. PL21: Ivy ... 3E 24
Edgar Ter. PL4: Plym ... 4F 19
Edgcumbe Av. PL1: Plym ... 6A 18
Edgcumbe Cres. PL10: Mill ... 3C 26
Edgcumbe Dr. PL19: Tavi ... 2D 36
Edgcumbe Pk. Rd. PL3: Plym ... 2C 18
Edgcumbe St. PL1: Plym ... 7K 17
Edgecumbe Ho. PL1: Plym ... 5A 4
Edgecumbe Rd. PL12: Salt ... 2K 9
Edinburgh St. PL1: Dev ... 7H 17
Edith Av. PL4: Plym ... 5F 19
Edith St. PL5: Plym ... 6G 11
Edna Ter. PL4: Plym ... 6G 19
Edwards Cl. PL7: Plymp ... 4J 21
Edwards Cres. PL12: Salt ... 5K 9
Edwards Dr. PL7: Plymp ... 3J 21
Effingham Cres. PL3: Plym ... 1C 18
EFFORD ... 3H 19
Efford Crematorium
PL3: Plym ... 2H 19
Efford Cres. PL3: Plym ... 2G 19
Efford La. PL3: Plym ... 4G 19
Efford Marshes Local Nature Reserve
... 2K 19
Efford Pathway PL3: Plym ... 2H 19
Efford Rd. PL3: Plym ... 2G 19
Efford Wlk. PL3: Plym ... 2G 19
Egerton Cres.
PL4: Plym ... 3K 5 (6F 19)
Egerton Pl. PL4: Plym ... 3K 5 (6F 19)
Egerton Rd. PL4: Plym ... 4J 5 (6E 18)
EGGBUCKLAND ... 7G 13
Eggbuckland Rd. PL3: Plym ... 2E 18
PL6: Plym ... 7G 13
Egret Cl. PL10: Mill ... 3D 26
Eight Acres Cl. PL7: Plymp ... 3K 21
Elaine Cl. PL7: Plymp ... 3C 20
Elbow La. PL19: Tavi ... 2E 36
Elbridge Cotts. PL8: Brixt ... 4H 31
ELBURTON ... 2D 30
Elburton Rd. PL9: Elb, Plyms ... 1B 30
Eldad Hill PL1: Plym ... 3A 4 (6A 18)
Elder Cl. PL7: Plymp ... 3J 21
Elford Cres. PL7: Plymp ... 1F 21
Elford Dr. PL9: Plyms ... 2H 29
Elfordleigh Golf Course ... 5G 15
Elford Pk. PL20: Yelv ... 6D 38
Elgin Cres. PL5: Plym ... 4D 12
Elim Ct. PL3: Plym ... 3D 18
Elim Ter. PL3: Plym ... 3D 18
Eliot St. PL5: Plym ... 7H 11
Elizabethan House ... 6F 5
Elizabeth Cl. PL21: Ivy ... 3G 25
Elizabeth Pl.
PL4: Plym ... 2F 5 (5D 18)
Elliot Sq. PL11: Torp ... 5E 16
Elliot St. PL1: Plym ... 7C 4 (1B 28)
Elliott Cl. PL12: Salt ... 5A 10
Elliot Ter. PL1: Plym ... 7D 4
Elliot Ter. La.
PL1: Plym ... 7D 4 (1C 28)
Elliott Rd. PL4: Plym ... 7F 19
Elliott's Grocery Store ... *5D 10*
(off Lwr. Fore St.)
Elliotts Hill PL8: Brixt ... 5H 31
Elm Cl. PL19: Tavi ... 5E 36
Elm Cotts. *PL12: Salt ... 4K 9*
(off Thorn La.)
Elm Cres. PL3: Plym ... 4F 19
Elm Cft. *PL6: Plym ... 1J 13*
(off Elm Rd.)
Elmcroft PL2: Plym ... 1A 18
ELMGATE ... 7F 9
Elm Gro. PL6: Plym ... 7G 13
PL7: Plymp ... 3F 21
Elm Pk. PL10: Mill ... 2E 26
Elm Rd. PL4: Plym ... 3E 18
PL6: Plym ... 1J 13
Elms, The PL3: Plym ... 5K 17
Elm Ter. *PL4: Plym ... 3E 18*
(off Elm Rd.)
Elm Tree Cl. PL8: Yeal ... 5C 32
Elm Tree Pk. PL8: Yeal ... 5C 32
Elmwood Cl. PL6: Plym ... 2J 13
Elphinstone Rd. PL2: Plym ... 1B 18
Elwell Rd. PL12: Salt ... 4D 10
Elwick Gdns. PL3: Plym ... 3G 19
Embankment La. PL4: Plym ... 6G 19
Embankment Rd. PL3: Plym ... 6G 19
PL4: Plym ... 5K 5 (7F 19)
Embankment Rd. La. Nth.
PL4: Plym ... 6G 19
(off Grenville Rd.)
Emily Gdns. PL4: Plym ... 1J 5 (5E 18)
Emma Pl. PL1: Plym ... 7K 17
Emma Pl. Ope PL1: Plym ... 7K 17
Endeavour Ct. PL1: Plym ... 5K 17
Endsleigh Gdns.
PL4: Plym ... 2F 5 (5D 18)
Endsleigh Pk. Rd. PL3: Plym ... 2C 18
Endsleigh Pl.
PL4: Plym ... 2F 5 (5D 18)
Endsleigh Rd. PL9: Plyms ... 2H 29
Endsleigh Vw. PL21: Ivy ... 3B 24
Eningdale Rd. PL19: Tavi ... 4C 36
Ennerdale Gdns. PL6: Plym ... 3D 12
Enterprise Ct. PL11: Torp ... 6F 17
Epping Cres. PL6: Plym ... 1J 19
Epworth Ter. PL2: Plym ... 3J 17
Eric Rd. PL4: Plym ... 4K 5 (6F 19)
Erith Av. PL2: Plym ... 1J 17
Erle Gdns. PL7: Plymp ... 5G 21
Erlstoke Cl. PL6: Plym ... 6J 13
Erme Ct. PL21: Ivy ... 3E 24
Erme Dr. PL21: Ivy ... 3D 24
Erme Gdns. PL3: Plym ... 3H 19
Erme M. PL21: Ivy ... 4D 24
Erme Rd. PL21: Ivy ... 3E 24
Erme Ter. PL21: Ivy ... 3E 24
Ermington Rd. PL21: Ivy ... 4C 24
Ermington Ter. PL4: Plym ... 4D 18
ERNESETTLE ... 3H 11
Ernesettle Cres. PL5: Plym ... 4H 11
Ernesettle Grn. PL5: Plym ... 3H 11
Ernesettle La. PL5: Plym ... 2G 11
Ernesettle Rd. PL5: Plym ... 4H 11
Ernesettle Ter. *PL5: Plym ... 4H 11*
(off Ernesettle Rd.)
Erril Retail Pk. PL7: Plymp ... 3C 20
Esmonde Gdns. PL5: Plym ... 7E 10
Esplanade, The
PL1: Plym ... 7D 4 (1C 28)
ESSA ... 5C 10
Essa Rd. PL12: Salt ... 5C 10
Essex St. PL1: Plym ... 2B 4 (5B 18)
Esso Wharf Rd.
PL4: Plym ... 7K 5 (1F 29)
ESTOVER ... 4K 13
Estover Cl. PL6: Plym ... 3A 14
Estover Ind. Est. PL6: Plym ... 3A 14
Estover Rd. PL6: Plym ... 3K 13
Estuary Way PL5: Plym ... 7F 11
Eton Av. PL1: Plym ... 2D 4 (5C 18)
Eton Pl. PL1: Plym ... 2D 4 (5C 18)
Eton St. PL1: Plym ... 3D 4 (5C 18)
Eton Ter. PL1: Plym ... 3C 4 (6B 18)
Evans Pl. PL2: Plym ... 3A 18
Evelyn Pl. PL4: Plym ... 1F 5 (5D 18)
Evelyn St. PL5: Plym ... 6G 11
Evenden Ct. PL11: Torp ... 5D 16
Exchange St. PL4: Plym ... 6F 5
Exe Gdns. PL3: Plym ... 1H 19
Exeter Cl. PL5: Plym ... 3G 11
Exeter Rd. PL21: Fil, Ivy ... 3E 24
Exeter St. PL4: Plym ... 5F 5 (6D 18)
Exmouth Rd. PL1: Dev ... 5J 17
(not continuous)
Explorer Ct. PL2: Plym ... 3A 18

F

Fairfax Ter. PL2: Plym ... 4J 17
Fairfield PL7: Plymp ... 1F 21
Fairfield Av. PL2: Plym ... 1B 18
Fairmead M. PL12: Salt ... 4K 9
Fairmead Rd. PL12: Salt ... 5K 9
Fairview Av. PL3: Plym ... 3J 19
Fairview Way PL3: Plym ... 3K 19
Fairway PL12: Salt ... 5K 9
Fairway, The PL8: New F ... 5G 35
Fairway Av. PL21: Ivy ... 3C 24
Falcon Rd. PL1: Dev ... 7J 17
Fanshawe Way PL9: Hooe ... 3H 29
Faraday Mill Bus. Pk.
PL4: Plym ... 7G 19
Faraday Mill Trade Pk.
PL4: Plym ... 7G 19
Faraday Rd. PL4: Plym ... 7G 19
Faringdon Rd. PL4: Plym ... 5G 19
Farm Cl. PL7: Plymp ... 2D 20
Farm La. PL5: Plym ... 5A 12
PL6: Plym ... 7G 13
PL12: Salt ... 6A 10
Farnley Cl. PL6: Plym ... 1G 13
Farriers Cotts. PL7: Plymp ... 2F 21
Fayre Vw. PL12: T'han ... 6H 9
Fearnside Way PL12: Salt ... 4K 9
Federation Rd. PL3: Plym ... 4H 19
Fegen Rd. PL5: Plym ... 6E 10

Fellowes La.—Greenbank

Fellowes La. PL1: Plym 5A 18
Fellowes Pl. PL1: Plym 6K 17
Fellowes Pl. La. Sth.
PL1: Plym 6A 18
(off Edgcumbe Av.)
Fenten Pk. PL12: Salt 4C 10
Fernbank Av. PL21: Ivy 2B 24
Fern Cl. PL7: Plymp 3J 21
Ferndale Av. PL2: Plym 1H 17
Ferndale Cl. PL6: Plym 6J 7
Ferndale Rd. PL2: Plym 1H 17
Fernhill Cl. PL21: Ivy 3C 24
Fernleigh Rd. PL3: Plym 3E 18
Fern Mdw. PL19: Tavi 2F 37
Ferrers Rd. PL5: Plym 6H 11
Ferry La. PL11: Torp 2A 16
Ferry Rd. PL1: Dev 5G 17
Ferry St. PL11: Torp 5F 17
Feversham Cl. PL7: Plymp 2J 21
FILHAM 4G 25
Filham Ind. Est. *PL21: Ivy 3E 24*
(off Blair Rd.)
Filham Moor Cl. PL21: Ivy 4F 25
Fillace La. PL20: Horr 2B 38
Fillace Pk. PL20: Horr 2B 38
Fillham Moor La. PL21: Ivy 3E 24
Fincer Dr. PL21: Ivy 2B 24
Finch Cl. PL3: Plym 4J 19
Finches Cl. PL9: Elb 2D 30
Findon Gdns. PL6: Plym 3J 13
Finewell St.
PL1: Plym 5E 4 (7C 18)
Finnigan Rd. PL4: Plym 1G 29
Fircroft Rd. PL2: Plym 1A 18
Firestone Cl. PL6: Plym 6K 13
First Av. PL1: Dev 6K 17
PL9: Plyms 1A 30
Firtree Ri. PL21: Ivy 3E 24
Firtree Rd. *PL6: Plym 1K 13*
(off Glenfield Way)
Fisgard Way PL11: Torp 5A 16
Fisher Rd. PL2: Plym 3K 17
Fish Quay PL4: Plym 6H 5
Fistral Cl. PL11: Torp 4C 16
Fitzford Cotts. PL19: Tavi 4C 36
Fitzroy Rd. PL1: Plym 5K 17
Fitzroy Ter. PL1: Plym 5K 17
Flagstaff Wlk. PL1: Dev 7J 17
Flamborough Rd. PL6: Plym 7F 7
Flamborough Way
PL6: Plym 1F 13
Flamsteed Cres. PL5: Plym 6H 11
Fleet St. PL2: Plym 2H 17
Fleetwood Gdns. PL6: Plym 7F 7
Fletcher Cres. PL9: Plyms 3B 30
Fletcher Way PL9: Plyms 3B 30
Fletemoor Rd. PL5: Plym 6G 11
Flete Vw. Ter. PL21: Bitta 6K 25
Flora Cotts.
PL1: Plym 5B 4 (7B 18)
Flora Ct. PL1: Plym 4B 4 (6B 18)
(not continuous)
Flora St. PL1: Plym 5B 4 (7B 18)
Florence Pl. PL4: Plym 6F 19
Florence St. PL5: Plym 6G 11
Florida Gdns. PL3: Plym 2H 19
Floyd Cl. PL2: Plym 1J 17
Foliot Av. PL2: Plym 2K 17
Foliot Rd. PL2: Plym 1J 17
FORD
PL2 . . . . .3K 17
PL8 . . . . .7K 33
Fordbrook La. PL8: Brixt 5E 30
PL9: Brixt, Spri 6C 30
Ford Cl. PL21: Ivy 3B 24
FORDER 6K 9
Forder Hgts. PL6: Plym 6G 13
Forder Hill PL10: Caws, Rame . . .7C 26
Forder Valley Local Nature Reserve
. . . . .7J 13
Forder Valley Rd. PL6: Plym 6G 13
Ford Hill PL2: Plym 3K 17
FORD PARK 3C 18
Ford Pk. PL4: Plym 4D 18
Ford Pk. La. PL4: Plym 4D 18
Ford Pk. Rd. PL4: Plym 4C 18
Ford Rd. PL8: Torr 6D 32
PL9: Wem 3A 34
Ford St. PL19: Tavi 3D 36
Forest Av. PL2: Plym 1B 18
Foresters Rd. PL9: Plyms 2J 29
Fore St. PL1: Dev 6H 17
PL5: Tam F 1A 12
PL7: Plymp 4F 21
PL8: Yeal 5C 32
PL10: K'and 7D 26
PL10: Mill 4B 26
PL11: Torp 5E 16
PL12: Salt 5C 10
PL21: Ivy 3D 24
Forest Vw. PL6: Plym 7J 7
Forge Cl. PL6: Robo 5H 7
Forge La. PL12: Salt 3K 9
Forresters Bus. Pk.
PL6: Plym 2A 14
Forresters Dr. PL6: Plym 7J 7
Forsythia Dr. PL12: Salt 4J 9
Fort, The PL10: Caws 7D 26
Fort Austin Av. PL6: Plym 5E 12
Fort Bovisand 7E 28
Fortescue Pl. PL3: Plym 2F 19
Fortescue Ter. PL19: Tavi 2C 36
Forth Gdns. PL3: Plym 2J 19
Fort Stamford Health & Fitness Cen.
. . . . .3F 29
Fort Stamford The Ramparts
PL9: Hooe 3F 29
Fort Ter. PL6: Plym 4E 12
Fosbrooke Ct. PL3: Plym 2E 18
Foulston Av. PL5: Plym 7E 10
Foundry La. PL8: Noss M 7G 35
Foundry M. PL19: Tavi 2F 37
Fountains Cres. PL2: Plym 7A 12
Fowey Gdns. PL3: Plym 2J 19
Fox Fld. Cl. PL3: Plym 3H 19
Foxglove Way PL12: Salt 4J 9
Foxtor Cl. PL5: Plym 4A 12
Foxwood Gdns. PL6: Plym 2D 12
PL9: Plyms 4K 29
Foyle Cl. PL7: Plymp 3H 21
Francis Pl. PL1: Plym 3A 4 (6A 18)
Francis St. PL1: Plym 4A 4 (6A 18)
Frankfort Ga.
PL1: Plym 4C 4 (6B 18)
Franklyns PL6: Plym 3F 13
Franklyns Cl. PL6: Plym 3F 13
Fraser Pl. PL5: Tam F 7B 6
Fraser Rd. PL5: Tam F 7B 6
Fraser Sq. PL5: Tam F 6B 6
Frederick St. E.
PL1: Plym 4B 4 (6B 18)
Frederick St. W.
PL1: Plym 4B 4 (6B 18)
Fredington Gro. PL2: Plym 2A 18
Freedom Sq.
PL4: Plym 1H 5 (5E 18)
Freeman's Wharf PL1: Plym 1K 27
Freemantle Gdns. PL2: Plym 4J 17
Fremantle Pl. PL2: Plym 4J 17
Frenchman's La.
PL12: L'ake, N'ter 1C 8
Frensham Av. PL6: Plym 1H 13
Frensham Gdns. PL6: Plym 7H 7
Freshford Cl. PL6: Plym 6H 13
Freshford Wlk. PL6: Plym 6H 13
Frewin Gdns. PL6: Plym 1G 13
Friars La. PL1: Plym 6F 5
Friars Wlk. PL19: Whitc 6G 37
Friary Pk. PL4: Plym 4J 5 (6E 18)
Friary St. PL4: Plym 5H 5 (7E 18)
Frith Rd. PL12: Salt 4A 10
Frobisher App. PL5: Plym 5C 12
Frobisher Dr. PL12: Salt 5B 10
Frobisher Way PL11: Torp 5A 16
PL19: Tavi 3D 36
Frogmore Av. PL6: Plym 1G 19
(not continuous)
Frogmore Ct. PL6: Plym 1G 19
Frome Cl. PL7: Plymp 4H 21
Frontfield Cres. PL6: Plym 2D 12
Fullerton Rd. PL2: Plym 3K 17
Furland Cl. PL9: Hooe 4H 29
Furneaux Av. PL2: Plym 3A 18
Furneaux Rd. PL2: Plym 3A 18
Fursdon Cl. PL9: Elb 3D 30
Furse Pk. PL5: Plym 1F 17
Furzeacre Cl. PL7: Plymp 1H 21
Furzehatt Av. PL9: Plyms 3B 30
Furzehatt Pk. Rd. PL9: Plyms . . .3B 30
Furzehatt Ri. PL9: Plyms 3B 30
Furzehatt Rd. PL9: Plyms 3A 30
Furzehatt Vs. PL9: Plyms 3A 30
Furzehatt Way PL9: Plyms 3B 30
Furzehill Rd.
PL4: Plym 1H 5 (4E 18)

G

Gala Bingo
Plymouth, Charles Cross . . .4F 5
Plymouth, Derry's Cross . . .5C 4
Galileo Cl. PL7: Plymp 2F 21
Gallacher Way PL12: Salt 4J 9
Gallops, The PL12: Salt 3A 10
Galsworthy Cl. PL5: Plym 5B 12
Galva Rd. PL7: Drak, Hem 7K 15
Ganges Rd. PL2: Plym 3K 17
Ganna Pk. Rd. PL3: Plym 2C 18
Gara Cl. PL9: Elb 3C 30
Garden Cl. PL7: Plymp 3A 22
Garden Cres.
PL1: Plym 7B 4 (1B 28)
Garden La. PL19: Tavi 3D 36
Garden Pk. Cl. PL9: Elb 2C 30
Garden St. PL2: Dev 4H 17
Garden Village PL9: Plyms 1A 30
Gards La. PL5: Plym 5H 11
Garfield Ter. PL1: Plym 5J 17
Garrett St. PL10: Caws 7D 26
Garrick Cl. PL5: Plym 5B 12
Garrison Cl. PL1: Dev 7H 17
Garrison Grn. PL1: Plym 6F 5
Garston Cl. PL9: Plyms 1B 30
Gascoyne Ct. PL4: Plym 4G 5
Gascoyne Pl.
PL4: Plym 4G 5 (6D 18)
Gashouse La.
PL4: Plym 6J 5 (7E 18)
Gasking St. PL4: Plym . . .4G 5 (6D 18)
Gdynia Way PL4: Plym . . .5K 5 (7F 19)
Geasons La. PL7: Plymp 3F 21
Geffery Cl. PL12: L'ake 1B 8
George Av. PL7: Plymp 2F 21
George Junction
(Park & Ride) 1H 13
George La. PL7: Plymp 3G 21
George Pl. PL1: Plym 5A 4 (7A 18)
George Sq. *PL1: Dev 7J 17*
(off Theatre Ope)
George St. PL1: Dev 7J 17
George St. La. E. PL1: Dev 7J 17
Georgia Cres. PL3: Plym 2H 19
Gibbon La.
PL4: Plym 3F 5 (6D 18)
Gibbon St. PL4: Plym 3F 5 (6D 18)
Gifford Pl. PL3: Plym 4C 18
Gifford Ter. Rd. PL3: Plym 3C 18
Gilbert Ct. PL7: Plymp 2J 21
Gilbert La. PL2: Plym 3B 18
Gillard Way PL21: L Mill 3K 23
Gill Pk. PL3: Plym 3G 19
Gilston Rd. PL12: Salt 3K 9
Gilwell Av. PL9: Plyms 2B 30
Gilwell Hall PL4: Plym 3F 5
Gilwell Pl. PL4: Plym 3F 5 (6D 18)
Gilwell St. PL4: Plym 3G 5 (6D 18)
Gipsy La. PL21: Ivy 3A 24
Glade, The PL20: C'stone 6A 38
Glade Cl. PL6: Plym 3F 13
Glanville Rd. PL19: Tavi 3D 36
Glanvilles Mill PL21: Ivy 3D 24
Glanvilles Rd. PL21: Ivy 3E 24
Glanville St. PL4: Plym . . .3E 4 (6C 18)
Glanville Ter. PL12: Salt 3C 10
Glebe Av. PL12: Salt 4C 10
Glenavon Rd. PL3: Plym 3D 18
GLENBOURNE UNIT 4G 13
Glenburn Cl. PL3: Plym 1D 18
Glendower Rd. PL3: Plym 3C 18
Gleneagle Av. PL3: Plym 2E 18
Gleneagle Rd. PL3: Plym 2E 18
Gleneagle Vs. *PL3: Plym 2E 18*
(off Gleneagle Av.)
Glenfield Cl. PL6: Plym 1J 13
Glenfield Rd. PL6: Plym 2H 13
Glenfield Way PL6: Plym 1J 13
Glenhaven Cl. PL7: Plymp 2K 21
GLENHOLT 1J 13
Glenholt Cl. PL6: Plym 1J 13
Glenholt Pk. PL6: Plym 1J 13
Glenholt Rd. PL6: Plym 1H 13
Glenhurst Rd. PL3: Plym 2D 18
Glenmore Av. PL2: Plym 3J 17
Glen Pk. Av. PL4: Plym . . .1E 4 (5C 18)
Glen Rd. PL3: Plym 3E 18
PL7: Plymp 2E 20
Glenside *PL5: Plym 5D 12*
(off Whitleigh Av.)
Glenside Ri. PL7: Plymp 2F 21
Glentor Rd. PL3: Plym 1D 18
Glenwood Rd. PL3: Plym 2D 18
Globe Theatre 7K 17
Gloucester Ct. PL1: Plym 2D 4
Gloucester Pl.
PL1: Plym 2D 4 (5C 18)
Goad Av. PL4: Plym 7F 19
PL11: Torp 5B 16
Goad Cl. PL11: Torp 5C 16
Godding Gdns. PL6: Plym 7D 6
Godwell La. PL21: Ivy 5E 24
Golden Sq. PL7: Plymp 2F 21
Goldfinch Gdns. PL19: Whitc 6F 37
Goldfinch Gro. PL12: Salt 3A 10
Goldsmith Gdns. PL5: Plym 4C 12
Golf Links Rd. PL20: Yelv 7C 38
Goodeve Cl. PL9: Plyms 3K 29
Goodwin Av. PL6: Plym 1F 13
Goodwin Cres. PL2: Plym 2K 17
Gooseberry La.
PL1: Plym 6C 4 (7B 18)
GOOSEWELL 4A 30
Goosewell Hill PL6: Plym 7G 13
Goosewell Pk. Rd.
PL9: Plyms 3A 30
Goosewell Rd. PL9: Plyms 3A 30
Goosewell Ter. PL9: Plyms 3A 30
Gordon Ct. PL12: Salt 5A 10
Gordon Ter. PL4: Plym . . .1F 5 (4D 18)
PL10: Mill 4C 26
Gorse Way PL21: Ivy 4E 24
Gorsey Cl. PL5: Plym 5D 12
Goswela Cl. PL9: Plyms 4A 30
Goswela Gdns. PL9: Plyms 4A 30
GOVERMELIN 4B 26
Gower Ridge Rd. PL9: Plyms . . .3J 29
Grafton Rd. PL4: Plym 4D 18
Grainge Rd. PL6: Plym 6F 13
Granby Ct. PL1: Dev 6H 17
Granby Grn. PL1: Dev 6H 17
Granby Pl. PL1: Dev 6H 17
Granby St. PL1: Dev 5H 17
Granby Way PL1: Dev 6H 17
Grand Hotel Rd.
PL1: Plym 7C 4 (1B 28)
Grand Pde. PL1: Plym . . .7C 4 (1B 28)
Grange Rd. PL7: Plymp 4G 21
PL20: Yelv 5C 38
Grantham Cl. PL7: Plymp 4C 20
Grantley Gdns. PL3: Plym 4F 19
Grasmere Cl. PL6: Plym 2D 12
Grassendale Av. PL2: Plym 1J 17
Grass La. PL2: Plym 2B 18
Grassmere Way PL12: Salt 3A 10
Grassy La. PL8: Wors 2H 33
Gratton La. PL20: Yelv 7D 38
Gratton Pl. PL6: Plym 6F 13
Gravesend PL11: Torp 5E 16
Gravesend Gdns. PL11: Torp 5E 16
Gravesend Wlk. PL5: Plym 3G 11
Graybridge Rd. PL20: Horr 2B 38
Gray Cres. PL5: Plym 7F 11
Gt. Berry Rd. PL6: Plym 6E 12
Great Churchway PL9: Plyms . . .2B 30
Greatfield Rd. PL3: Plym 1G 19
Greatlands Cres. PL2: Plym 2K 17
Greatlands Pl. PL2: Plym 2K 17
Gt. Mis Tor Cl. PL20: Yelv 5C 38
Gt. Orchard Cl. PL9: Plyms 4K 29
Great Pk. Cl. PL7: Plymp 3K 21
Gt. Western Rd.
PL1: Plym 7B 4 (1B 28)
Gt. Woodford Dr.
PL7: Plymp 2C 20
Grebe Cl. PL7: Plymp 3G 21
Green, The PL5: Plym 4H 11
PL8: New F 5H 35
PL9: Hooe 3G 29
PL10: K'and 7D 26
PL12: Salt 4K 9
PL20: Horr 2B 38
(off Jordan La.)
Greenacres PL9: Plyms 1A 30
Greenbank PL4: Plym 1H 5

A-Z Plymouth 45

Greenbank Av.—Hollacombe Brake

Greenbank Av. PL4: Plym 2J 5 (5E 18)
Greenbank Cotts. PL4: Plym 1H 5
PL7: Plymp 4E 20 (off Underwood Rd.)
Greenbank Ct. PL4: Plym 2H 5
Greenbank Rd. PL4: Plym 1H 5 (5E 18)
Greenbank Ter. PL4: Plym 2H 5 (5E 18)
PL20: Yelv 6D 38
Greendale Rd. PL2: Plym 1K 17
Greenfield Dr. PL21: Ivy 4E 24
Greenfield Rd. PL12: Salt 5A 10
Greenfinch Cres. PL12: Salt 3A 10
Green Hill PL19: Tavi 2F 37
Greenhill Cl. PL9: Plyms 4A 30
Greenhill Rd. PL9: Spri 5B 30
Greenland PL10: Mill 4B 26
Greenlands Est. PL19: Tavi 3F 37
Green La. PL10: K'and 7D 26 (off Fore St.)
PL19: Tavi 3F 37
PL20: Yelv 7A 38
Greenlees Dr. PL7: Plymp 5J 21
Green Pk. PL10: Caws 7D 26
Green Pk. Av. PL4: Plym 1E 4 (4C 18)
Green Pk. Rd. PL9: Plyms 3J 29
Greens Cotts. PL12: T'han 6H 9
Green St. PL4: Plym 4F 5 (6D 18)
Greensway Rd. PL19: Tavi 4C 36
Greenway Av. PL7: Plymp 2C 20
Greenway Cl. PL20: Horr 1B 38
PL21: Ivy 3E 24
Greenwich Pl. PL12: Salt 4C 10 (off Glebe Av.)
Greenwood Cl. PL21: Ivy 3D 24
Greenwood Pk. Cl. PL7: Plymp 2J 21
Greenwood Pk. Rd. PL7: Plymp 2J 21
Grenfell Av. PL12: Salt 4K 9
Grenfell Gdns. PL12: Salt 4K 9
Grenville Battery 6E 26
Grenville Ct. PL7: Plymp 2K 21
Grenville Dr. PL19: Tavi 5D 36
Grenville Mdw. PL19: Tavi 5D 36
Grenville Pk. PL20: Yelv 6D 38
Grenville Rd. PL4: Plym 4J 5 (6E 18)
Grenville Rd. La. Sth. PL4: Plym 6G 19 (off Grenville Rd.)
Gresham Cl. PL5: Tam F 7B 6
Greystoke Av. PL6: Plym 1H 19
Griffin Way PL9: Elb 3D 30
Griggs Cl. PL7: Plymp 4J 21
Grimspound Cl. PL6: Plym 7K 13
Grizedale Rd. PL6: Plym 1J 19
Grosvenor Cotts. PL4: Plym 4E 18 (off Belgrave La.)
Grosvenor Ct. PL21: Ivy 3D 24
Grosvenor Rd. PL6: Plym 5E 12
Grove, The PL3: Plym 4K 17
PL9: Plyms 1J 29
PL21: Moor 6K 25
Grove Pk. PL11: Torp 5B 16
PL19: Tavi 3F 37
Groves, The PL21: Ivy 2D 24
Guildford Cl. PL5: Plym 4D 12
Guildford St. PL4: Plym 3G 5 (6D 18)
Guildhall Sq. PL1: Plym 5E 4 (7C 18)
Gun La. PL1: Dev 6H 17
Gunsey La. PL8: New F 4H 35
Gurnard Wlk. PL3: Plym 2J 19
Gurney Cl. PL11: Torp 5C 16
Guy Miles Way PL5: Plym 4A 12
Gwel Avon Bus. Pk. PL12: Salt 2A 10
Gwithian Cl. PL11: Torp 4C 16
Gwyn Rd. PL4: Plym 1K 5 (5F 19)

H

Haddington Rd. PL2: Dev 4H 17
Halcyon Ct. PL2: Plym 2K 17
Halcyon Rd. PL2: Plym 2K 17
Haldon Pl. PL5: Plym 4K 11
Hallerton Cl. PL6: Plym 6K 13
Hallett Cl. PL12: Salt 4J 9
Halley Gdns. PL5: Plym 6H 11
HAM 7K 11
Hamble Cl. PL3: Plym 1J 19
Ham Cl. PL2: Plym 7A 12
Ham Dr. PL2: Plym 1K 17
Ham Grn. PL2: Plym 1K 17
Ham Grn. Ct. PL2: Plym 1K 17
Ham Grn. La. PL2: Plym 1K 17
Hamilton Gdns. PL4: Plym 1E 4 (4C 18)
Ham La. PL2: Plym 6J 11
PL5: Plym 6J 11
Hamoaze Av. PL5: Plym 7G 11
Hamoaze Ct. PL1: Dev 7H 17
Hamoaze Pl. PL1: Dev 6G 17
Hamoaze Rd. PL11: Torp 6E 16
Ham Pl. PL2: Plym 7K 11
Hampton St. PL4: Plym 4F 5 (6D 18)
Ham Woods Local Nature Reserve 6K 11
Hancock Cl. PL6: Plym 1C 12
Hannaford Rd. PL8: Noss M 7G 35
Hanover Cl. PL3: Plym 3H 19
Hanover Ct. PL1: Plym 6F 5
Hanover Rd. PL3: Plym 3G 19
Harbour Av. PL4: Plym 5G 5 (7D 18)
PL5: Plym 7H 11
Harbourside Ct. PL4: Plym 5G 5
Harbour St. PL11: Torp 5E 16
Harbour Vw. PL9: Hooe 2F 29
PL12: Salt 5B 10 (off Higher Port Vw.)
Harbour Vw. Rd. PL5: Plym 7H 11
Hardings Cl. PL12: Salt 3B 10
Hardwick Farm PL7: Plymp 5D 20
Hardy Cres. PL5: Plym 6D 12
Harebell Cl. PL12: Salt 3K 9
Hareston Cl. PL7: Plymp 5J 21
Harewood Cl. PL7: Plymp 3E 20
Harewood Cres. PL5: Plym 5K 11
Harford Rd. PL21: Harf, Ivy 3E 24
Hargood Ter. PL2: Dev, Plym 4J 17
Hargreaves Cl. PL5: Plym 5J 11
Harlech Cl. PL3: Plym 1F 19
Harnorlen Rd. PL2: Plym 1C 18
Haroldsleigh Av. PL5: Plym 5D 12
Harriet Gdns. PL7: Plymp 2C 20
Harris Ct. PL9: Hooe 3G 29
Harrison St. PL2: Dev 4J 17
Harris Way PL21: L Mill 4G 23
Harrowbeer La. PL20: Yelv 4C 38
Harrowbeer M. PL20: Yelv 6C 38
Hartland Cl. PL6: Plym 7F 7
HARTLEY 1D 18
Hartley Av. PL3: Plym 2E 18
Hartley Ct. PL3: Plym 2F 19
PL21: Ivy 3D 24
Hartley Pk. Gdns. PL3: Plym 2E 18
Hartley Rd. PL3: Plym 2D 18
HARTLEY VALE 7F 13
Hartwell Av. PL9: Elb 2E 30
Harvey Av. PL4: Plym 7G 19
Harvey St. PL11: Torp 5E 16
Harwell Ct. PL1: Plym 4C 4 (6B 18)
Harwell St. PL1: Plym 3C 4 (6B 18)
Harwood Av. PL5: Tam F 7B 6
Hastings St. PL1: Plym 3C 4 (6B 18)
Hastings Ter. PL1: Plym 3C 4 (6B 18)
Haswell Cl. PL6: Plym 7F 13
Hat La. PL10: Caws 7C 26
Hatshill Cl. PL6: Plym 4B 14
Havelock Ter. PL2: Dev 5J 17
Hawarden Cotts. PL4: Plym 7G 19 (off Cavendish Rd.)
Haweswater Cl. PL6: Plym 3D 12
Hawkers Av. PL4: Plym 5G 5 (7D 18)
Hawkers La. PL3: Plym 3D 18
Hawkinge Gdns. PL5: Plym 3H 11
Hawkins Cl. PL6: Plym 2F 13
Hawks Pk. PL12: Salt 5K 9
Hawthorn Av. PL11: Torp 5C 16
Hawthorn Cl. PL6: Plym 7J 7
PL9: Hooe 4H 29
Hawthorn Dr. PL9: Wem 4B 34
Hawthorne Wlk. PL21: L Mill 4G 23 (off Holly Berry Rd.)
Hawthorn Gro. PL2: Plym 1B 18
Hawthorn Pk. Rd. PL9: Wem 4B 34
Hawthorn Rd. PL19: Tavi 6E 36
Hawthorns PL12: Salt 5A 10
Hawthorn Way PL3: Plym 1G 19
Haxter Cl. PL6: Robo 5G 7
Haydon Gro. PL5: Plym 6F 11
Haye Rd. PL9: Elb 6C 20
Haye Rd. Sth. PL9: Elb 2D 30
Hayes Pl. PL6: Plym 7G 13
Hayes Rd. PL9: Plyms 2H 29
Haystone Pl. PL1: Plym 2B 4 (5B 18)
Haytor Cl. PL5: Plym 4A 12
Haytor Dr. PL21: Ivy 4E 24
Hazelbank Ct. PL5: Plym 6E 10
Hazel Cl. PL6: Plym 1G 13
Hazeldene Cl. PL21: L Mill 4G 23
Hazel Dr. PL9: Elb 2D 30
Hazel Gro. PL9: Elb 2D 30
PL20: Yelv 5D 38
Hazel Rd. PL19: Tavi 6E 36
Hazelwood Cres. PL9: Elb 2E 30
Hazelwood Dr. PL6: Plym 6J 7
Headland Pk. PL4: Plym 1G 5 (5D 18)
Healy Pl. PL2: Dev 5H 17
Heanton Ter. PL10: Mill 3C 26
Hearl Rd. PL12: Salt 4J 9
Heather Cl. PL19: Tavi 4F 37
Heather M. PL21: Ivy 3D 24
Heathers, The PL6: Plym 7J 7
Heather Wlk. PL21: Ivy 4E 24
Heathfield Pk. PL20: Dous 4E 38
Heathfield Rd. PL4: Plym 5G 19
Heavitree Rd. PL10: K'and 7D 26
Hedgerow Cl. PL6: Plym 6K 7
Hedgerows, The PL12: Salt 4J 9
Hedingham Cl. PL7: Plymp 4K 21
Hedingham Gdns. PL6: Plym 7G 7
Heights, The PL19: Tavi 2C 36
Hele Gdns. PL7: Plymp 4G 21
Heles Ter. PL4: Plym 6G 19
HEMERDON 1K 21
Hemerdon Hgts. PL7: Plymp 2H 21
Hemerdon La. PL7: Hem, Plymp 7J 15
Hemerdon Vs. PL7: Plymp 2F 21 (off Colebrook Rd.)
Hemerdon Way PL7: Plymp 2E 20
Henderson Pl. PL2: Plym 2J 17
Hendwell Cl. PL6: Plym 1D 12
Henlake Cl. PL21: Ivy 2C 24
Henley Dr. PL5: Tam F 7B 6
Henry Cl. PL21: L Mill 4G 23
Hensbury La. PL20: Bere F 1A 6
Herbert Pl. PL2: Dev 4H 17
Herbert St. PL2: Dev 4H 17
Hereford Rd. PL5: Plym 2A 12
Heritage Cl. PL12: Salt 4K 9
Heritage Pk. PL19: Tavi 2F 37
Hermitage Ct. PL4: Plym 4D 18
Hermitage Rd. PL3: Plym 3D 18
Hern La. PL8: Yeal 5C 32
Heron Cl. PL10: Mill 3C 26
Herschel Gdns. PL5: Plym 6H 11
Hertland Wlk. PL2: Plym 1K 17
Hessary Dr. PL6: Robo 6H 7
Hessary Vw. PL12: Salt 4B 10
PL19: Tavi 2D 36
Hetling Cl. PL1: Plym 3B 4 (6B 18)
Hewers Row PL4: Plym 4G 5 (6D 18)
Hewitt Cl. PL12: Salt 6K 9
Hexham Pl. PL2: Plym 7K 11
HEXTON 3H 29
Hexton Hill Rd. PL9: Hooe 3G 29
Hexton Quay 3G 29
Heybrook Av. PL5: Plym 6G 11
Hibernia Ter. PL5: Plym 7H 11
Hickory Dr. PL7: Plymp 3J 21
Hicks La. PL4: Plym 5F 5 (7D 18)
High Acre Dr. PL21: Ivy 2B 24
Highbank Cl. PL19: Tavi 4C 36
Highbridge Ct. PL7: Plymp 3F 21 (off Ridgeway)
Highbury Cres. PL7: Plymp 1E 20
Highclere Gdns. PL6: Plym 6G 7
Highcombe La. PL9: Bovis 5H 29
Higher Anderton Rd. PL10: Mill 4C 26
Higher Brook Pk. PL21: Ivy 3B 24
Higher Churchway PL9: Plyms 2B 30
HIGHER COMPTON 2F 19
Higher Compton Rd. PL3: Plym 2E 18
Higher Efford Rd. PL3: Plym 3G 19
HIGHER KEATON 7E 24
Higher La. PL1: Plym 5E 4
Higher Mowles PL3: Plym 2G 19
Higher Pk. Cl. PL7: Plymp 5J 21
Higher Port Vw. PL12: Salt 5B 10
Higher Row PL10: K'and 7D 26 (off Devonport Hill)
Higher Stert Ter. PL4: Plym 6F 19
Highertown PL20: Horr 1B 38
Highertown Pk. PL12: L'ake 1C 8
Higher Woodford La. PL7: Plymp 1D 20
Highfield Cl. PL3: Plym 3H 19
Highfield Dr. PL9: Wem 3B 34
Highfield Pk. PL12: Salt 4J 9
Highfield Ter. PL21: Bitta 7K 25
Highglen Dr. PL7: Plymp 1J 21
Highlands PL8: Yeal 5C 32
Highland St. PL21: Ivy 3D 24
High Rd. PL9: Wem 3A 34
High St. PL1: Plym 5F 5 (Buckwell St.)
PL1: Plym 7K 17 (Edgcumbe St.)
Hill Cl. PL7: Plymp 4E 20
Hill Ct. M. PL10: Mill 4B 26
Hill Crest PL3: Plym 3D 18
Hillcrest Cl. PL7: Plymp 3H 21
PL9: Wem 4B 34
Hillcrest Dr. PL7: Plymp 4H 21
Hilldale Rd. PL9: Plyms 3K 29
Hilldean Cl. PL5: Tam F 7B 6
Hillhead PL8: Noss M 6G 35
Hill La. PL3: Plym 1E 18
Hill Pk. Cres. PL4: Plym 1G 5 (5D 18)
Hill Pk. M. PL4: Plym 1H 5 (5E 18)
Hill Path PL5: Plym 2J 11
Hillsborough PL4: Plym 4E 18
Hillsdunne Rd. PL3: Plym 2D 18
Hillside PL21: Bitta 6K 25
Hillside Av. PL4: Plym 4C 18
PL12: Salt 4C 10
Hillside Cotts. PL8: Noss M 7G 35
Hillside Ct. PL7: Plymp 2F 21
Hillside Cres. PL9: Plyms 1A 30
Hillside Dr. PL8: Torr 6C 32
Hillside Rd. PL12: Salt 4B 10
Hillside Way PL8: Torr 6D 32
Hill St. PL4: Plym 4G 5 (6D 18)
Hilltop Cotts. PL8: Brixt 4G 31
Hill Top Crest PL5: Plym 5H 11
Hilton Av. PL5: Plym 6B 12
Hingston Ct. PL6: Plym 7F 13
Hinton Ct. PL6: Plym 6H 13
Hirmandale Rd. PL5: Plym 4J 11
HM Dockyard PL1: Dev 6G 17
HM Dockyard Nth. PL2: Dev 2F 17
HM Dockyard Sth. PL1: Dev 7G 17
Hobart St. PL1: Plym 5A 4 (7A 18)
Hobbs Cres. PL12: Salt 4K 9
Hodge Cl. PL12: Salt 5K 9
HOE, THE 7D 4 (1C 28)
Hoe App. PL1: Plym 6E 4 (7C 18)
Hoe Ct. PL1: Plym 6D 4
Hoe Gdns. PL1: Plym 6E 4
Hoegate Ct. PL1: Plym 6E 4
Hoegate Pl. PL1: Plym 6E 4
Hoegate St. PL1: Plym 6F 5 (7D 18)
Hoe Park 6D 4 (1C 28)
Hoe Rd. PL1: Plym 7C 4 (1C 28)
Hoe St. PL1: Plym 6E 4 (7C 18)
Hogarth Cl. PL9: Elb 3C 30
Hogarth Ho. PL19: Tavi 2E 36 (off Taylor Sq.)
Hogarth Wlk. PL9: Elb 3C 30
HOLBETON 7K 33
Holborn Pl. PL7: Plymp 2F 21
Holborn St. PL4: Plym 5J 5 (7E 18)
Holcombe Dr. PL9: Plyms 4A 30
Holcroft Cl. PL12: Salt 5A 10
Holdsworth St. PL4: Plym 1C 4
Holebay Cl. PL9: Plyms 4B 30
Hollacombe Brake PL9: Wem 1C 34

Hollacombe Hill—Lamerton Cl.

HOLLACOMBE HILL 7B 30
Holland Rd. PL3: Plym 2D 18
PL7: Plymp 3K 21
PL9: Plyms 3A 30
Holloway Gdns. PL9: Plyms 4B 30
Hollowgutter La. PL11: Torp 6A 16
Hollow Hayes *PL6: Plym 7G 13*
(off Goosewell Hill)
Hollows, The PL9: Elb 1C 30
Holly Berry Rd. PL21: L Mill 4G 23
Holly Ct. PL6: Plym 1K 19
Hollycroft Rd. PL3: Plym 1F 19
Holly Pk. Cl. PL5: Plym 2K 11
Holly Pk. Dr. PL5: Plym 2K 11
Hollywood Ter. PL1: Plym 3A 4
Holman Ct. PL2: Plym 7B 12
Holmans Bldgs. PL1: Dev 6G 17
Holman Way PL21: Ivy 2B 24
Holmbush Way PL8: Brixt 5H 31
Holmer Down PL6: Plym 7J 7
Holmes Av. PL3: Plym 3G 19
Holmwood Av. PL9: Plyms 4K 29
Holne Chase PL6: Plym 7G 7
Holtwood Dr. PL21: Ivy 3B 24
Holtwood Rd. PL6: Plym 1J 13
Holwell Cl. PL9: Plyms 4B 30
Holyrood Pl.
PL1: Plym 7D 4 (1C 28)
Home Farm Rd. PL9: Plyms 1K 29
Home Park 3B 18
Home Pk. PL2: Dev 4J 17
PL12: L'ake 1B 8
Home Pk. Av. PL3: Plym 2D 18
Home Pk. Rd. PL12: Salt 4D 10
Homer Pk. PL9: Hooe 4H 29
PL12: Salt 4A 10
Homer Pk. La. Sth.
PL9: Hooe 4H 29
Homer Ri. PL9: Elb 2C 30
Home Sweet Home Ter.
PL4: Plym 6K 5 (7F 19)
Honcray PL9: Plyms 1J 29
Honeysuckle Cl. PL6: Plym 7K 7
PL12: Salt 3A 10
HONICKNOWLE 5B 12
Honicknowle Grn. PL5: Plym 4A 12
Honicknowle La. PL2: Plym 6A 12
PL5: Plym 6A 12
Honiton Cl. PL5: Plym 4A 12
Honiton Wlk. PL5: Plym 3A 12
HOOE 3G 29
Hooe Hill PL9: Hooe 4H 29
Hooe Lake PL10: Mill 5E 26
Hooe La. PL9: Stad 5H 29
Hooe Rd. PL9: Hooe 3G 29
Hooksbury Av. PL7: Plymp 5J 21
Hoopers Cl. PL12: L'ake 2B 8
Hooper St. PL11: Torp 5F 17
Hopton Cl. PL6: Plym 7E 12
Hornbrook Gdns. PL6: Plym 1C 12
Hornby St. PL2: Plym 4J 17
Hornchurch La. PL5: Plym 3H 11
Hornchurch Rd. PL5: Plym 2H 11
Horn Cross Rd. PL9: Plyms 2K 29
Horn La. PL8: Brixt 4H 31
PL9: Plyms 2K 29
Horn La. Flats PL9: Plyms 2A 30
HORRABRIDGE 2B 38
Horseshoe Dr. PL7: Plymp 3E 20
Horsham La. PL5: Plym 5B 12
PL5: Tam F 6A 6
Horswell Cl. PL7: Plymp 3J 21
Hosford Cl. PL9: Plyms 5A 30
Hospital Rd.
PL4: Plym 2H 5 (5E 18)
Hotham Pl. PL1: Plym 2A 4 (5A 18)
Houldsworth Rd. PL9: Plyms 2H 29
Houndiscombe Rd.
PL4: Plym 1F 5 (5D 18)
Hounster Dr. PL10: Mill 5A 26
Hounster Hill PL10: Mill 4A 26
Housman Cl. PL5: Plym 4C 12
Howard Cl. PL5: Plym 5J 11
PL12: Salt 4A 10
PL19: Tavi 3C 36
Howard Ct. PL1: Plym 7B 4
Howard Rd. PL9: Plyms 1K 29
Howards Way PL21: Ivy 2B 24
Howeson La. PL6: Plym 3F 13
How St. PL4: Plym 5F 5 (7D 18)
Hub, The PL2: Plym 1K 17
Humber Cl. PL3: Plym 2J 19
Hungerford Rd. PL2: Plym 2A 18
Hunsdon Rd. PL21: Ivy 5A 24
Hunter Cl. PL6: Plym 5E 12
Hunters Cl. PL21: Ivy 3C 24
Huntingdon Gdns. PL5: Plym 3C 12
Huntley Pl. PL3: Plym 4H 19
Huntley Vs. PL3: Plym 4H 19
Hurdwick Rd. PL19: Tavi 3C 36
Hurrabrook Cl. PL6: Plym 5K 13
Hurrabrook Gdns. PL6: Plym 5K 13
Hurrell Cl. PL6: Plym 1C 12
Hurrell Ct. PL3: Plym 3H 19
Hursley Bus. Pk. PL6: Robo 5K 7
Hurst Cl. PL9: Plyms 4A 30
Hutchings Cl. PL6: Plym 1C 12
Huxham Cl. PL6: Plym 7F 13
Huxley Cl. PL7: Plymp 1G 21
Hyde Pk. Rd. PL3: Plym 3D 18

I

Ice Rink
Plymouth 5B 4 (7B 18)
Ilbert St. PL1: Plym 2C 4 (5B 18)
Ince Cl. PL11: Torp 4B 16
Inchkeith Rd. PL6: Plym 1E 12
Ingra Rd. PL3: Plym 2F 19
Ingra Tor PL20: Yelv 5C 38
Ingra Wlk. PL6: Robo 6G 7
Instow Wlk. PL5: Plym 4K 11
Inswell Ct. PL19: Tavi 2C 36
INSWORKE 3C 26
Insworke Cl. PL10: Mill 3D 26
Insworke Cres. PL10: Mill 3C 26
Insworke Pl. PL10: Mill 3D 26
Inverdene PL3: Plym 3C 18
Ipswich Cl. PL5: Plym 3B 12
Ivanhoe Rd. PL5: Plym 5G 11
IVYBRIDGE 3E 24
Ivybridge (Park & Ride) 3G 25
Ivybridge Leisure Centre &
Outdoor Pool 4E 24
Ivybridge Rd. PL21: Erm 7F 25
Ivybridge Station (Rail) 2G 25
Ivybridge Viaduct 1E 24
Ivydale Rd. PL4: Plym 4E 18
Ivydene Rd. PL21: Ivy 3C 24

J

Jackmans Mdw. PL10: Caws 7D 26
Jackson Cl. PL5: Plym 7H 11
Jackson Pl. PL2: Dev 4J 17
Jackson Way PL12: Salt 4B 10
Jago Av. PL11: Torp 5D 16
James Cl. PL9: Elb 2C 30
James Rd. PL19: Whitc 6G 37
James St. PL1: Dev 7H 17
PL4: Plym 3E 4 (6C 18)
Janeva Ct. PL12: Salt 4K 9
Jasmine Gdns. PL6: Plym 1K 13
PL7: Plymp 3J 21
Jean Cres. PL3: Plym 2G 19
Jedburgh Cres. PL2: Plym 7K 11
Jefferson Wlk.
PL3: Plym 1C 4 (5B 18)
Jeffery Cl. PL6: Plym 1C 12
Jellicoe Rd. PL5: Plym 6D 12
Jenkins Cl. PL9: Plyms 4B 30
Jennycliff La. PL9: Hooe 4F 29
Jennyscombe Cl. PL9: Plyms 5A 30
Jephson Rd. PL4: Plym 5G 19
Jessops PL7: Plymp 1E 20
Jinkin Av. PL4: Plym 1J 5 (5E 18)
John Gaynor Homes PL4: Plym 4G 5
Johnston Ter. Ope PL2: Plym 2H 17
Jordan La. PL20: Horr 2B 38
Jubilee Cl. PL12: Salt 5A 10
PL21: Ivy 2G 25
Jubilee Cotts. *PL6: Plym 7G 13*
(off Church Hill)
PL12: Salt 6A 10
Jubilee Pl. *PL3: Plym 4H 19*
(off Huntley Pl.)
Jubilee Rd. PL5: Plym 4J 11
Jubilee Ter. *PL4: Plym 6G 19*
(off Brentor Rd.)
PL21: Bitta 7J 25
Julian Pl. PL2: Plym 3J 17
Julian Rd. PL21: Ivy 3C 24
Julian St. PL4: Plym 6K 5 (7F 19)
Julian Wlk. PL6: Plym 1K 13
Jump Cl. PL6: Robo 5H 7
Junction Gdns. PL4: Plym 6F 19
Juniper Way PL7: Plymp 3J 21

K

Kathleaven St. PL5: Plym 6G 11
Kay Cl. PL7: Plymp 1G 21
Keast M. *PL12: Salt 5C 10*
(off Fore St.)
Keaton La. PL21: Erm, Ivy 5E 24
Keaton Rd. PL21: Ivy 4D 24
Keat St. PL2: Dev 4H 17
Kedlestone Av. PL5: Plym 4K 11
Keep, The PL12: Salt 5K 9
Kelly Cl. PL5: Plym 1F 17
Kelvin Av. PL4: Plym 1K 5 (5F 19)
Kempe Cl. PL2: Plym 2J 17
Kempton Ter. PL11: Torp 5E 16
Kemyell Pl. PL2: Dev 4H 17
Kendal Pl. PL5: Plym 3D 12
Kenilworth Rd. PL2: Plym 1A 18
Kenley Gdns. PL5: Plym 3J 11
Kenmare Dr. PL7: Plymp 3H 21
Kenn Cl. PL5: Plym 4A 12
Kennel Hill PL7: Plymp 4E 20
Kennel Hill Cl. PL7: Plymp 4D 20
Kennel La. PL21: Ivy 3B 24
Kennels, The PL21: Ivy 2C 24
Kennet Cl. PL3: Plym 2G 19
Kensington Pl. PL4: Plym 4E 18
Kensington Rd.
PL4: Plym 1H 5 (4E 18)
Kent Rd. PL2: Plym 3J 17
Keppel Pl. PL2: Dev 4J 17
Keppel St. PL2: Dev 4J 17
Keppel Ter. *PL2: Dev 4J 17*
(off Keppel St.)
Kernow Cl. PL11: Torp 5B 16
Ker St. PL1: Dev 7H 17
Ker St. Ope PL1: Dev 6H 17
Kestor Cl. PL2: Plym 1K 17
Kestral Pk. PL5: Plym 6K 11
Kestrel Pk. PL19: Whitc 6F 37
Kestrel Way PL6: Plym 6J 7
Keswick Cres. PL6: Plym 5J 13
Keyes Cl. PL1: Dev 6J 17
KEYHAM 2H 17
Keyham Rd. PL2: Dev 4H 17
Keyham Station (Rail) 2H 17
Keyham St. PL5: Plym 7H 11
Khyber Cl. PL11: Torp 5D 16
Kidwelly Cl. PL7: Plymp 4K 21
Kiel Pl. PL3: Plym 3J 19
Kiel Pl. La. PL3: Plym 3J 19
Killigrew Av. PL12: Salt 6A 10
Kiln Cl. PL5: Plym 7F 11
Kilnpark Wlk. PL11: Torp 2A 16
Kilworthy Hill PL19: Tavi 2E 36
Kilworthy Pk. PL19: Tavi 2E 36
Kilworthy Rd. PL19: Tavi 2E 36
Kimberley Cotts.
PL12: Salt 4K 9
(off Thorn La.)
Kimberly Dr. PL6: Plym 6G 13
Kingdom Pl. PL12: Salt 5C 10
King Edward Rd. PL12: Salt 5C 10
Kingfisher Cl. PL6: Plym 1K 13
PL19: Whitc 6E 36
Kingfisher Way PL9: Plyms 2H 29
King Gdns. PL1: Plym 3C 4
KINGSAND 7D 26
Kings Cl. PL6: Plym 1K 13
Kings Ct. PL1: Dev 5K 17
Kingsland Gdn. Cl.
PL3: Plym 2D 18
Kingsley Av. PL11: Torp 6E 16
Kingsley Cl. PL21: L Mill 4K 23
Kingsley Rd. PL4: Plym 4D 18
Kingsmill Rd. PL12: Salt 2A 10
Kings Rd. PL1: Dev 6J 17
PL5: Plym 4J 11
KING'S TAMERTON 6J 11
King's Tamerton Rd.
PL5: Plym 5H 11
Kingston Cl. PL7: Plymp 3H 21
Kingston Dr. PL7: Plymp 2H 21
King St. PL1: Plym 4A 4 (6A 18)
PL10: Mill 4B 26
PL11: Torp 5F 17
PL19: Tavi 2D 36
Kingsway PL7: Plymp 3B 22
PL10: K'and 7E 26
Kingsway Gdns. PL6: Plym 4E 12
Kingswear Cres. PL6: Plym 6G 13
Kingswood Pk. Av. PL3: Plym 2C 18
Kinnaird Cres. PL6: Plym 7D 6
Kinross Av. PL4: Plym 1K 5 (4F 19)
Kinsale Rd. PL5: Plym 4J 11
Kinterbury Rd. PL5: Plym 7E 10
Kinterbury St.
PL1: Plym 5F 5 (7D 18)
Kinterbury Ter. PL5: Plym 7E 10
Kinver Cl. PL6: Plym 3J 13
Kipling Gdns. PL5: Plym 5C 12
Kirkby Pl. PL4: Plym 2E 4 (5C 18)
Kirkby Ter. PL4: Plym 2E 4
Kirkdale Gdns. PL2: Plym 1A 18
Kirkella Rd. PL20: Yelv 6D 38
Kirkland Cl. PL6: Plym 7H 7
Kirkstall Cl. PL2: Plym 1J 17
Kirkwall Rd. PL5: Plym 4D 12
(not continuous)
Kirton Pl. PL3: Plym 3G 19
Kit Hill Cres. PL5: Plym 7F 11
Kitley Pl. PL8: Yeal 5B 32
Kitley Vw. PL8: Brixt 4J 31
Kitley Way PL5: Plym 6H 11
Kitter Dr. PL9: Plyms 4A 30
Knapps Cl. PL9: Elb 3D 30
Kneele Gdns. PL3: Plym 7D 12
KNIGHTON 2C 34
Knighton Hill PL9: Wem 2D 34
Knighton Hill Bus. Cen.
PL9: Wem 2D 34
Knighton Rd. PL4: Plym 4J 5 (6E 18)
PL9: Wem 2C 34
Knighton Ter. PL20: Horr 1B 38
Knill Cross PL10: Mill 4B 26
Knoll, The PL7: Plymp 2C 20
Knowland Cl. PL1: Dev 6J 17
Knowle Av. PL2: Plym 2H 17
Knowle Wlk. PL2: Plym 2J 17
Kynance Cl. PL11: Torp 4C 16

L

Labatt Cl. PL6: Plym 4J 13
Laburnum PL19: Tavi 2E 36
Laburnum Dr. PL9: Wem 3B 34
Laburnum Gro. *PL6: Plym 2J 13*
(off Beech Ct.)
Lady Fern Rd. PL6: Robo 5H 7
Ladysmith Ct.
PL4: Plym 1K 5 (5F 19)
Ladysmith Rd.
PL4: Plym 1K 5 (5F 19)
Ladywell Av. PL4: Plym 3G 5
Ladywell Pl.
PL4: Plym 3G 5 (6E 18)
LAIRA 4H 19
Laira Av. PL3: Plym 4J 19
Laira Bridge 7H 19
Laira Bri. Rd. PL4: Plym 6G 19
Laira Gdns. PL3: Plym 4H 19
Laira Pk. Cres. PL4: Plym 4G 19
Laira Pk. Pl. PL4: Plym 4G 19
Laira Pk. Rd. PL4: Plym 4G 19
Laira Pl. PL4: Plym 4K 5 (6F 19)
Laira St. PL4: Plym 4K 5 (6F 19)
Laity Wlk. PL6: Plym 1C 12
Lake La. PL20: Dous 5E 38
Lake M. PL10: Mill 4B 26
Lake Rd. PL9: Hooe 3G 29
Lakeside PL19: Tavi 2D 36
Lakeside Dr. PL5: Plym 2G 11
Lake Vw. Cl. PL5: Plym 1A 12
Lake Vw. Dr. PL5: Plym 2K 11
Lalebrick Rd. PL9: Hooe 4F 29
Lambert Rd. *PL5: Tam F 1A 12*
(off Station Rd.)
Lambhay Hill
PL1: Plym 6F 5 (7D 18)
Lambhay St.
PL1: Plym 7F 5 (1D 28)
Lamerton Cl. PL5: Plym 4A 12

A-Z Plymouth 47

M

Redlake Trad. Est.—Saltash Leisure Cen.

Redlake Trad. Est.
PL21: Bitta 2J 25
Red Lion Hill PL8: Brixt 4H 31
Redmoor Cl. PL19: Tavi 1C 36
Redruth Cl. PL5: Plym 2K 11
Redvers Gro. PL7: Plymp 4F 21
Redwing Dr. PL6: Plym 6J 7
Redwood Dr. PL7: Plymp 3J 21
Reel Cinema
Plymouth 5D 4
Regent St. PL4: Plym . . . 3F 5 (6D 18)
Reigate Rd. PL9: Plyms 1K 29
Renaissance Gdns.
PL2: Plym 1B 18
Rendlesham Gdns. PL6: Plym . . . 4K 13
Rendlesham Rd. PL6: Plym . . . 4K 13
Rendle St. PL1: Plym . . . 4A 4 (6A 18)
Renney Rd. PL9: Down T 7H 29
Rennie Av. PL5: Plym 6F 11
Renoir Cl. PL9: Elb 3B 30
Renown St. PL2: Plym 2H 17
Research Way PL6: Plym 3H 13
Reservoir Cres. PL9: Elb 2C 30
Reservoir La. PL3: Plym 2E 18
Reservoir Rd. PL3: Plym 2E 18
PL9: Elb 3C 30
Reservoir Way PL9: Elb 2C 30
Resolution Ho. PL4: Plym 4H 5
Restormel Rd.
PL4: Plym 1E 4 (5C 18)
Restormel Ter. PL4: Plym 1E 4
Retreat, The PL3: Plym 1G 19
Revell Pk. Rd. PL7: Plymp 2E 20
Revel Rd. PL3: Plym 2F 19
Revelstoke Rd. PL8: Noss M . . . 6G 35
Reynolds Gro. PL5: Plym 7F 11
Reynolds Rd. PL7: Plymp 2D 20
Rheola Gdns. PL6: Plym 4J 13
Rhodes Cl. PL7: Plymp 1F 21
Ribble Gdns. PL3: Plym 1J 19
Richardson Dr. PL8: Yeal 3K 35
Richards Row PL3: Plym 1E 18
Richards Ter. PL10: Mill 4B 26
Richmond Rd. PL6: Plym 5F 13
Richmond Wlk. PL1: Dev 1H 27
Ride, The PL9: Plyms 7H 19
Ridge Ho. PL4: Plym 1K 5 (4F 19)
Ridge Pk. PL7: Plymp 3F 21
Ridge Pk. Av.
PL4: Plym 1E 4 (4C 18)
Ridge Pk. Rd. PL7: Plymp 3F 21
Ridge Rd. PL7: Plymp 5D 20
Ridgeway PL7: Plymp 3E 20
PL12: Salt 6A 10
Ridgeway Community Sports Cen.
. . . . . 3F 21
Rifleman Wlk. PL6: Plym 7G 7
Riga Ter. PL3: Plym 4H 19
Rigdale Cl. PL6: Plym 1F 19
Ringmore Way PL5: Plym 3K 11
Risdon Av. PL4: Plym 7G 19
Riverbank PL12: Salt 4D 10
River Ct. PL12: Salt 2A 10
PL19: Tavi 2F 37
Riverford PL6: Plym 2A 14
Riverford Cl. PL6: Plym 7J 7
River Pk. PL20: Horr 2C 38
Rivers, The PL12: Salt 6B 10
Rivers Cl. PL21: Ivy 3F 25
RIVERSIDE 5E 10
Riverside Bus. Pk. PL1: Dev . . . 5H 17
Riverside Caravan Pk.
PL6: Plym 7A 14
Riverside Cl. PL20: Horr 2B 38
Riverside Cotts. PL12: Salt 6K 9
Riverside M. PL12: Salt 4D 10
Riverside Pl. *PL1: Dev 6G 17*
(off Cannon St.)
Riverside Rd. E. PL8: New F . . . 6G 35
Riverside Rd. W. PL8: New F . . . 6G 35
Riverside Wlk. PL5: Tam F 1A 12
PL8: Torr 5D 32
Riversleigh PL3: Plym 3K 19
River Vw. PL4: Plym 7G 19
PL12: Salt 4C 10
River Vw. La. PL4: Plym 7F 19
RIXHILL 7D 36
Robbins Hall PL4: Plym 3F 5
Robert Adams Cl. PL7: Plymp . . . 3B 20
Roberts Av. PL11: Torp 5E 16
Roberts Rd. PL5: Plym 7F 11
Robins Way PL9: Plyms 1K 29
ROBOROUGH 5H 7
Roborough Av. PL6: Plym 2G 13
Roborough Cl. PL6: Plym 2G 13
Roborough Down La.
PL6: Robo 1K 7
Roborough La. PL5: Tam F 6B 6
(Allern La.)
PL5: Tam F 5E 6
(Soper's Hill)
PL6: Robo 5E 6
Robyns Cl. PL7: Plymp 3J 21
Rochester Rd.
PL4: Plym 1G 5 (5D 18)
Rochford Cres. PL5: Plym 2J 11
Rockdale Rd. PL8: Torr 6D 32
Rockfield Av. PL6: Plym 1E 12
Rock Gdns. PL9: Plyms 7J 19
Rock Hill PL5: Tam F 7B 6
Rockingham Rd. PL3: Plym 3F 19
Rock Ter. PL7: Plymp 4E 20
Rockville Pk. PL9: Plyms 1K 29
Rockwood Rd. PL6: Plym 6K 7
Rocky Hill PL19: Tavi 3D 36
Rocky Pk. Av. PL9: Plyms 1K 29
Rocky Pk. Rd. PL9: Plyms 2K 29
Roddick Way PL7: Plymp 3K 21
Rodney St. PL5: Plym 7G 11
Roeselare Av. PL11: Torp 5D 16
Roeselare Cl. PL11: Torp 5D 16
Rogate Dr. PL6: Plym 3J 13
Rogate Wlk. PL6: Plym 3J 13
Rogers Dr. PL12: Salt 3A 10
Roland Bailey Gdns.
PL19: Tavi 2C 36
Roland Matthews Ct.
PL2: Dev 4H 17
(off Boscawen Pl.)
Rollis Pk. Cl. PL9: Plyms 1H 29
Rollis Pk. Rd. PL9: Plyms 1H 29
Rolston Cl. PL6: Plym 1C 12
Roman Rd. PL5: Plym 6H 11
Roman Way PL5: Plym 5H 11
Romilly Gdns. PL7: Plymp 3C 20
Romney Cl. PL5: Plym 6A 12
Ronald Ter. PL2: Plym 3J 17
Ronsdale Cl. PL9: Plyms 1J 29
Roope Cl. PL5: Plym 1F 17
Roper Av. PL9: Plyms 1J 29
Rope Wlk. PL4: Plym 6G 5 (7E 18)
Rope Walk, The
PL4: Plym 7K 5 (1F 29)
Rorkes Cl. PL5: Plym 5H 11
Rosebery Av.
PL4: Plym 2K 5 (5F 19)
Rosebery La.
PL4: Plym 1K 5 (5F 19)
Rosebery Rd.
PL4: Plym 2K 5 (5F 19)
Roseclave Cl. PL7: Plymp 2K 21
Rose Cotts. PL6: Plym 7G 13
Rosedale Av. PL2: Plym 1C 18
Rosedown Av. PL2: Plym 1K 17
Rose Gdns. PL6: Plym 1J 13
Rose Hill PL9: Wem 4B 34
Rosehip Cl. PL6: Plym 7K 7
Rosevean Ct. PL3: Plym 2E 18
Rosevean Gdns. PL3: Plym 2E 18
Roseveare Cl. PL9: Plyms 1B 30
Rose Vs. PL21: Bitta 6J 25
Rosewood Cl. PL9: Plyms 4A 30
Rospeath Cres. PL2: Plym 7C 12
Rosslyn Pk. Rd. PL3: Plym 3C 18
Ross St. PL2: Dev 4H 17
(not continuous)
Rothbury Cl. PL6: Plym 3K 13
Rothbury Gdns. PL6: Plym 3J 13
Rothesay Gdns. PL5: Plym 4B 12
Rougemont Cl. PL3: Plym 1G 19
Roundsnest PL8: Torr 6C 32
Rowan Cl. PL7: Plymp 3J 21
PL19: Tavi 5E 36
Rowan Ct. PL12: Salt 5K 9
Rowan Way PL6: Plym 7K 7
Rowden St. PL3: Plym 3D 18
Row Down Cl. PL7: Plymp 4A 22
Rowe St. PL11: Torp 5E 16
Rowland Cl. PL9: Hooe 4K 29
Row La. PL5: Plym 5H 11
Royal Albert Bridge 5D 10
Royal Albert Ct. PL12: Salt 4A 10
Royal Citadel, The 7F 5 (1D 28)
ROYAL EYE INFIRMARY 3G 13
Royal Naval War Memorial
. . . . . 7D 4 (1C 28)
Royal Navy Av. PL2: Plym 3H 17
Royal Pde. PL1: Plym . . . 5D 4 (7C 18)
Royal Plymouth Corinthian Yacht Club
. . . . . 7F 5 (1D 28)
Royal William Rd. PL1: Plym . . . 1K 27
Royal William Yard 2K 27
Royal William Yd. PL1: Plym . . . 2K 27
Rudyerd Wlk. PL3: Plym 2H 19
Rue St Pierre PL21: Ivy 3F 25
Rufford Cl. PL2: Plym 1K 17
Runnymede Ct. PL6: Plym 5K 13
Runway Rd. PL6: Plym 2G 13
Ruskin Cres. PL5: Plym 5C 12
Russell Av. PL3: Plym 1E 18
Russell Cl. PL9: Plyms 2C 30
PL12: Salt 4K 9
Russell Ct. PL19: Tavi 2D 36
Russell Ct. Gdns. PL19: Tavi . . . 2D 36
Russell Pl. PL4: Plym . . . 1D 4 (5C 18)
Russell St. PL19: Tavi 3E 36
Russet Wood PL5: Plym 3J 11
Rutger Pl. PL1: Plym 5A 18
Ruthven Cl. PL6: Plym 7E 12
Rutland Rd. PL4: Plym 4E 18
Rutt La. PL21: Ivy 2G 25
Rydal Cl. PL6: Plym 5J 13
Ryder Rd. PL2: Dev, Plym 3J 17
Rye Hill PL12: Salt 5K 9
Ryeland Cl. PL9: Wem 3C 34

S

St Aidan's Ct. PL5: Plym 2H 11
St Albans Pk. PL20: Yelv 6D 38
St Andrew's Cl. PL12: Salt 5K 9
St Andrews Cross
PL1: Plym 5E 4 (7C 18)
St Andrews Rd. PL19: Whitc . . . 6F 37
St Andrew's St. PL10: Caws . . . 7D 26
St Andrew St.
PL1: Plym 5E 4 (7C 18)
PL10: Mill 4A 26
St Anne's Rd. PL6: Plym 1J 13
PL12: Salt 4B 10
St Aubyn Av. PL2: Plym 3J 17
St Aubyn Rd. PL1: Dev 6H 17
St Aubyn St. PL1: Dev 6H 17
St Austin Cl. PL21: Ivy 3D 24
St Barnabas Ct.
PL1: Plym 2B 4 (5B 18)
ST BARNABAS HOSPITAL 5C 10
St Barnabas Ter.
PL1: Plym 2A 4 (5A 18)
St Boniface Cl. PL2: Plym 1B 18
St Boniface Dr. PL2: Plym 1B 18
St Bridget Av. PL6: Plym 6E 12
ST BUDEAUX 6G 11
St Budeaux By-Pass
PL5: Plym 7H 11
St Budeaux (Ferry Road) Station
(Rail) 7G 11
St Budeaux (Victoria Road) Station
(Rail) 6G 11
St Catherines Pk. PL8: New F . . . 5H 35
St Chad Cl. PL5: Plym 3B 12
St David's Rd. PL19: Tavi 4G 37
St Dunstan's Ter.
PL4: Plym 3K 5 (6F 19)
St Edward Gdns. PL6: Plym 6G 13
St Elizabeth Cl. PL7: Plymp . . . 4G 21
ST ERNEY 4B 8
St Erth Rd. PL2: Plym 1C 18
St Eval Pl. PL5: Plym 3H 11
St Francis Ct. PL5: Plym 4K 11
St Gabriel's Av. PL3: Plym 3C 18
St George's Av. PL2: Plym 1B 18
St George's Rd. PL12: Salt 4A 10
St George's Ter. PL2: Plym 4J 17
St Helen's Wlk. PL5: Plym 2B 12
St Hilary Ter.
PL4: Plym 3K 5 (6F 19)
St James Ct. PL1: Plym 6C 4
PL11: Torp 5E 16
St James M. PL1: Plym 6C 4
St James Pl. E.
PL1: Plym 6C 4 (7B 18)
St James Pl. W.
PL1: Plym 6C 4 (7B 18)
St James Rd. PL11: Torp 6E 16
St Johns PL19: Tavi 3E 36
St Johns Av. PL19: Tavi 3E 36
St John's Bri. Rd.
PL4: Plym 6J 5 (7E 18)
St Johns Cl. PL6: Plym 3J 13
PL10: Mill 4B 26
PL21: Ivy 3C 24
St Johns Ct. PL19: Tavi 4D 36
St John's Dr. PL9: Hooe 3G 29
St John's Rd.
PL4: Plym 5J 5 (7E 18)
PL9: Hooe 3F 29
PL10: Mill 3B 26
PL20: Horr 2B 38
PL21: Ivy 3C 24
St John's St. PL4: Plym . . . 5J 5 (7E 18)
St Johns Yd.
PL4: Plym 5H 5 (7E 18)
St Joseph's Cl. PL6: Plym 6E 12
ST JUDE'S 6G 19
St Judes Rd. PL4: Plym . . . 5J 5 (6E 18)
St Julian Cres. PL10: Crem 2H 27
St Keverne Pl. PL2: Plym 7C 12
St Lawrence M. PL4: Plym 1F 5
St Lawrence Rd.
PL4: Plym 1F 5 (5D 18)
St Leonards Rd.
PL4: Plym 5K 5 (7F 19)
St Leo Pl. PL2: Dev 4H 17
St Levan Rd. PL2: Plym 3H 17
ST LUKE'S HOSPICE PLYMOUTH
. . . . . 3F 29
St Margarets Rd. PL7: Plymp . . . 1C 20
St Market St. PL1: Plym 7K 17
St Marks Rd. PL6: Plym 2J 13
St Martin's Av. PL3: Plym 1C 18
St Maryhaye PL19: Tavi 3C 36
St Mary's Cl. PL7: Plymp 3E 20
St Mary's Ct. PL7: Plymp 3E 20
St Mary's Rd. PL7: Plymp 2D 20
St Mary St. PL1: Plym 6A 18
St Maurice M. PL7: Plymp 4F 21
St Maurice Rd. PL7: Plymp 5G 21
St Maurice Vw. PL7: Plymp 4J 21
St Mawes Ter. PL2: Plym 3J 17
St Michael Av. PL2: Plym 3J 17
St Michael's Cl. PL1: Dev 7H 17
St Michael's Ct. *PL1: Dev 5J 17*
(off Stopford Pl.)
St Michael's Ter. PL1: Dev 5J 17
St Michael's Ter. La.
PL4: Plym 2D 4 (5C 18)
St Modwen Rd. PL6: Plym 1K 19
St Nazaire App. PL1: Dev 6J 17
St Nazaire Cl. *PL1: Dev 6J 17*
(off St Nazaire App.)
St Pancras Av. PL2: Plym 6B 12
St Paul's Cl. PL3: Plym 3H 19
St Paul's Ct. *PL3: Plym 3H 19*
(off Torridge Way)
St Paul St. PL1: Plym 1K 27
St Peters Cl. PL7: Plymp 4G 21
St Peters Ct. PL1: Plym 4A 4
St Peters Rd. PL5: Plym 5B 12
St Peter's Way PL21: Ivy 4F 25
ST STEPHENS 6A 10
St Stephen's Hill PL12: Salt 6K 9
St Stephen's Pl. PL7: Plymp . . . 3F 21
St Stephen's Rd. PL7: Plymp . . . 5G 21
PL12: Salt 6A 10
St Stephen St. PL1: Dev 7J 17
St Teresa Ho. PL4: Plym 4G 5
St Theresa's Ct. *PL1: Dev 6J 17*
(off Raglan Rd.)
St Thomas Cl. PL7: Plymp 5G 21
St Thomas Ct. PL4: Plym 4G 5
St Vincent St. PL2: Plym 4H 17
St Werburgh Cl. PL9: Wem 4B 34
Salamanca St. PL11: Torp 5E 16
Salcombe Rd.
PL4: Plym 1J 5 (4E 18)
Salisbury Ope PL3: Plym 3A 18
Salisbury Rd.
PL4: Plym 3H 5 (6E 18)
SALTASH 5C 10
Saltash Bus. Pk. PL12: Salt 3K 9
Saltash By-Pass PL12: Salt 3J 9
Saltash Leisure Cen. 5B 10

52 A-Z Plymouth

Saltash Parkway Ind. Est.—Summerfields

Saltash Parkway Ind. Est.
PL12: Salt 3J 9
(Burraton Rd.)
PL12: Salt 3K 9
(Gilston Rd.)
Saltash Rd. PL2: Plym 3G 17
PL3: Plym 1C 4 (5C 18)
Saltash Sailing Club 5D 10
SALTASH SERVICE AREA 2K 9
Saltash Station (Rail) 5D 10
Saltburn Rd. PL5: Plym 5F 11
Saltmill Cl. PL12: Salt 4C 10
Saltmill Rd. PL12: Salt 3C 10
Saltram 4A 20
Saltram Ter. PL7: Plymp 3E 20
Sampford Gdns. PL20: Horr 1D 38
Sampford Ter. PL20: Horr 1C 38
Samuel Bassett Av. PL6: Plym 7G 7
Sanctuary Cl. PL2: Plym 3J 17
Sandford Rd. PL9: Plyms 1A 30
Sandon Wlk. PL6: Plym 7F 13
Sand Quay La. *PL12: Salt 5D 10*
(off Old Ferry Rd.)
Sandy La. PL21: Ivy 3E 24
Sandy Rd. PL7: Plymp 4K 21
Sango Ct. PL10: Mill 3C 26
Sango Rd. PL11: Torp 6D 16
San Sebastion Sq. PL1: Plym 5D 4
Sarum Cl. PL3: Plym 1E 18
Saunders Wlk. PL6: Plym 1C 12
Savage Rd. PL5: Plym 7F 11
Savery Cl. PL21: Ivy 2F 25
Savery Ter. PL4: Plym 4F 19
Sawrey St. PL1: Plym 5A 4 (7A 18)
Saxon Rd. PL19: Tavi 2C 36
School Cl. PL7: Plymp 1E 20
PL19: Tavi 3F 37
School Dr. PL6: Plym 7J 7
School La. PL7: Plymp 4F 21
School Rd. PL12: L'ake 1B 8
PL19: Whitc 6F 37
Sconner Rd. PL11: Torp 5D 16
Scott Av. PL5: Plym 7F 11
Scott Bus. Pk. PL2: Plym 2K 17
SCOTT HOSPITAL,
PLYMOUTH CHILD
DEVELOPMENT CENTRE 2K 17
Scott Memorial 7J 17
Scott Rd. PL2: Plym 2K 17
(Beacon Pk. Rd.)
PL2: Plym 3A 18
(Bowers Rd.)
Scotts Cotts. *PL9: Plyms 1J 29*
(off Millway Pl.)
Seacroft Rd. PL5: Plym 5F 11
Seaton Av. PL4: Plym 4D 18
Seaton Bus. Pk. PL6: Plym 4G 13
Seaton La. PL4: Plym 4D 18
Seaton Orchard PL7: Spa 1D 22
Seaton Pl. PL2: Plym 3J 17
Sea Vw. Av. PL4: Plym 1K 5 (5F 19)
Sea Vw. Dr. PL9: Wem 3B 34
Sea Vw. Ter. PL4: Plym 2J 5 (5E 18)
Second Av. PL1: Dev 6K 17
PL2: Plym 1H 17
PL9: Plyms 7B 20
Sedge Cl. PL21: Ivy 4E 24
Sedley Way PL5: Plym 4C 12
Sefton Av. PL4: Plym 4F 19
Sefton Cl. PL4: Plym 5F 19
Segrave Rd. PL2: Plym 3A 18
Selkirk Pl. PL5: Plym 5D 12
Sellon Ct. PL1: Plym 4C 4 (6B 18)
Selsden Cl. PL9: Elb 3D 30
Sendall's Way PL6: Plym 4E 12
Sennen Cl. PL11: Torp 4C 16
Sennen Pl. PL2: Dev 4H 17
Serpell Cl. PL6: Plym 1D 12
Seven Stars La. PL5: Tam F 1A 12
Seven Trees Ct.
PL4: Plym 1G 5 (5E 18)
Severn Pl. PL3: Plym 3H 19
Seymour Av. PL4: Plym 2J 5 (5E 18)
Seymour Dr. PL3: Plym 3E 18
Seymour Ho. PL1: Dev 7J 17
Seymour M. PL4: Plym 2K 5 (5F 19)
Seymour Pk. PL3: Plym 3F 19
Seymour Pl. PL1: Plym 2A 4 (5A 18)
Seymour Rd. PL3: Plym 3E 18
PL7: Plymp 2C 20
Seymour St.
PL4: Plym 3G 5 (6D 18)
Shackleton Ct. PL5: Plym 6C 12
Shaftesbury Cotts.
PL4: Plym 1G 5 (5D 18)
Shaftesbury Ct.
PL4: Plym 2G 5 (5D 18)
Shaftesbury Pl. *PL4: Plym 2G 5*
(off Shaftesbury Cotts.)
Shakespeare Rd. PL5: Plym 5A 12
Shaldon Cres. PL5: Plym 4A 12
Shallowford Cl. PL6: Plym 7H 13
Shallowford Rd. PL6: Plym 1H 19
Shapleys Gdns. PL9: Plyms 4B 30
Shapters Rd.
PL4: Plym 6K 5 (7F 19)
Sharon Way PL6: Plym 2F 13
Sharpitor Gdns. PL2: Plym 1K 17
Sharrose Rd. PL9: Hooe 4G 29
Shaw Way PL9: Hooe 2E 28
Shearwood Cl. PL7: Plymp 2D 20
Sheepstor Rd. PL6: Plym 6J 13
Shell Cl. PL6: Plym 6K 13
Shelley Av. PL19: Tavi 3F 37
Shelley Way PL5: Plym 6G 11
Shepherds La.
PL4: Plym 5H 5 (7E 18)
Sherborne Cl. PL9: Elb 3D 30
Sherford Cres. PL5: Plym 4K 11
PL9: Elb 2D 30
Sherford Proposed Development 7G 21
Sherford Rd. PL9: Elb 2D 30
Sherford Wlk. PL9: Elb 2F 31
Sheridan Rd. PL5: Plym 6B 12
Sherril Cl. PL9: Plyms 5A 30
Sherwell Arc. PL4: Plym 2F 5
Sherwell La.
PL4: Plym 2F 5 (5D 18)
Sherwill Cl. PL21: Ivy 2B 24
Shipley Wlk. PL6: Plym 6F 13
Shirburn Rd. PL6: Plym 6G 13
Shirley Gdns. PL5: Plym 6B 12
Shoemaker's La. PL12: Salt 5B 10
Short Cotts. PL11: Torp 5D 16
Short Pk. Rd. PL3: Plym 3C 18
Shortwood Cres. PL9: Plyms 2B 30
Shrewsbury Rd. PL5: Plym 3A 12
Shute Pk. Rd. PL9: Plyms 4A 30
Siding Rd. PL4: Plym 1D 4 (5C 18)
Sidmouth Cotts. PL4: Plym 1J 5
Silver Birch Cl. PL6: Plym 7H 7
Silver Stream Way PL8: Brixt 4J 31
Silver St. PL12: Salt 5D 10
Silver Ter. PL10: Mill 3D 26
Simon Cl. PL9: Plyms 3K 29
Sir John Hawkins Sq.
PL1: Plym 5F 5
Sir John Hunt Sports Cen. 3C 12
Sisna Pk. Rd. PL6: Plym 3K 13
Sithney St. PL5: Plym 6F 11
Six O'Clock La. PL7: Plymp 4F 21
Skardale Gdns. PL6: Plym 7J 13
Skardon Pl.
PL4: Plym 2F 5 (5D 18)
Skerries Rd. PL6: Plym 7E 6
Skylark Ri. PL6: Plym 6K 7
PL19: Whitc 7F 37
Slade Cl. PL9: Plyms 4B 30
Slatelands Cl. PL7: Plymp 5J 21
Slate La. PL1: Plym 7A 18
Slipperstone Dr. PL21: Ivy 2B 24
Smallack Cl. PL6: Plym 5E 12
Smallack Dr. PL6: Plym 5E 12
Smallridge Cl. PL9: Plyms 4A 30
Smeaton Sq. PL3: Plym 2J 19
Smeaton's Tower 7D 4 (1C 28)
SMITHALEIGH 5E 22
Smithaleigh Caravan & Camping Pk.
PL7: Smit 5E 22
Smithfield Dr. PL12: Salt 4J 9
Smiths Way PL12: Salt 4J 9
Smithy Cl. PL12: Salt 3K 9
Snell Dr. PL12: Salt 4J 9
Somerset Cotts. PL3: Plym 4K 17
Somerset Pl. PL3: Plym 4K 17
Somerset Pl. La. PL3: Plym 4K 17
Soper's Hill PL5: Tam F 5D 6
Sortridge Pk. PL20: Horr 1A 38
South Devon Tennis Cen. 4D 24
SOUTHDOWN 3E 26
Southdown Quay 3E 26
Sth. Down Rd. PL2: Plym 2A 18
Southdown Rd. PL10: Mill 3C 26
Sth. Down Ter. PL10: Mill 3D 26
Southella Rd. PL20: Yelv 6D 38
Southern Cl. PL2: Plym 1J 17
Southern Ter.
PL4: Plym 1H 5 (4E 18)
Southernway PL9: Plyms 2B 30
Southfield PL12: Salt 5K 9
Southgate Av. PL9: Plyms 4K 29
Southgate Cl. PL9: Plyms 4K 29
South Hill PL1: Plym 5K 17
PL9: Hooe 4H 29
Southland Pk. Cres.
PL9: Wem 3B 34
Southland Pk. Rd. PL9: Wem 4B 34
Sth. Milton St.
PL4: Plym 6K 5 (7F 19)
SOUTH PILL 3B 10
Southside Ope PL1: Plym 6F 5
Southside St.
PL1: Plym 6F 5 (7D 18)
South Vw. PL5: Plym 5D 12
PL7: Hem 1K 21
PL8: Brixt 4H 31
PL9: Elb 3C 30
PL20: Horr 2B 38
Southview PL10: Mill 3D 26
South Vw. Cl. PL7: Plymp 1E 20
South Vw. Pk. PL7: Plymp 1E 20
South Vw. Ter.
PL4: Plym 3K 5 (6F 19)
SOUTHWAY 7F 7
Southway Dr. PL6: Plym 2C 12
Southway La. PL6: Plym 1B 12
(Coombe La.)
PL6: Plym 7G 7
(Lulworth Dr.)
Southway Valley Local Nature Reserve 1E 12
Southwell Rd. PL6: Plym 7D 12
Southyard Way PL1: Dev 6H 17
Sovereign Ct. PL7: Plymp 3D 20
Sparke Cl. PL7: Plymp 4J 21
SPARKWELL 1C 22
Speakers Rd. PL21: Ivy 3F 25
Speares, The PL12: Salt 5J 9
Speculation Cotts. PL8: Yeal 5B 32
Speedwell Cl. PL10: Mill 4C 26
Speedwell Cres. PL6: Plym 1F 19
Speedwell Wlk. PL6: Plym 1G 19
Spencer Gdns. PL12: Salt 6B 10
Spencer Rd. PL9: Plyms 1K 29
Spinnaker Quay PL9: Hooe 2E 28
Spinney, The PL7: Plymp 4H 21
PL21: Ivy 3B 24
Spire Ct. PL3: Plym 2G 19
Spire Hill Pk. PL12: Salt 5K 9
SPRIDDLESTONE 5D 30
Springfield PL20: Horr 2C 38
Springfield Av. PL9: Elb 3C 30
Springfield Cl. PL9: Elb 3C 30
Springfield Dr. PL3: Plym 4K 17
Springfield La. PL9: Elb 2C 30
Springfield Ri. PL9: Elb 2C 30
Springfield Rd. PL9: Elb 3B 30
Spring Hill PL19: Tavi 3D 36
Springhill PL2: Plym 7B 12
Springhill Grn. PL2: Plym 7B 12
Spring Pk. PL6: Plym 7K 7
Springwood Cl. PL7: Plymp 5H 21
PL21: Ivy 3F 25
Spruce Gdns. PL7: Plymp 3J 21
Sprys Tenements PL20: Horr 1B 38
Square, The PL1: Plym 6K 17
PL12: Salt 4K 9
Squirrel Cl. PL5: Plym 3D 12
Stable Cotts. PL7: Plymp 3F 21
STADDISCOMBE 6K 29
Staddiscombe Rd.
PL9: Plyms, Stad 6K 29
Staddon Cres. PL9: Plyms 3K 29
Staddon Grn. PL9: Plyms 3J 29
Staddon Heights Golf Course 5F 29
Staddon La. PL9: Bovis 5G 29
Staddon Pk. Rd. PL9: Plyms 4K 29
Staddon Ter. La.
PL1: Plym 2C 4 (5B 18)
Stag La. PL9: Elb 1C 30
Stamford Cl. PL9: Hooe 3F 29
Stamford Fort Cotts.
PL9: Hooe 3F 29
(off Stamford Rd.)
Stamford La. PL9: Hooe 4F 29
Stamford Rd. PL9: Hooe 3F 29
Stamps Hill PL8: Brixt 3H 31
Stanborough Cross PL9: Elb 2D 30
Stanborough Rd.
PL9: Elb, Plyms 2A 30
Stanbury Av. PL6: Plym 6E 12
Standarhay Cl. PL9: Elb 2D 30
Standarhay Vs. PL9: Elb 2D 30
Stangray Av. PL4: Plym 4C 18
Stanhope Rd. PL5: Plym 5F 11
Staniforth Dr. PL21: Ivy 4E 24
Stanlake Cl. PL12: Salt 5A 10
Stanley Pl. PL4: Plym 6G 19
Stannary Bri. Rd. PL19: Tavi 2F 37
Stannary Cl. PL21: Ivy 3F 25
Stannary Ct. *PL19: Tavi 3D 36*
(off Garden La.)
Staple Cl. PL6: Robo 5H 7
Stapleford Gdns. PL5: Plym 2J 11
Station Rd. PL2: Plym 3H 17
PL5: Tam F 1H 11
PL7: Plymp 2F 21
PL9: Elb 2D 30
PL12: Salt 5D 10
PL20: Horr 2B 38
PL21: Ivy 2E 24
Steeple Cl. PL9: Plyms 5A 30
Steer Pk. Rd. PL7: Plymp 3K 21
Steer Point Cotts. PL8: Brixt 7G 31
Steer Point Rd. PL8: Brixt 5H 31
Stefan Cl. PL9: Hooe 4G 29
Stenlake Pl. *PL4: Plym 6G 19*
(off Stenlake Ter.)
Stenlake Ter. PL4: Plym 6G 19
Stentaway Cl. PL9: Plyms 1A 30
Stentaway Dr. PL9: Plyms 1A 30
Stentaway Rd. PL9: Plyms 2A 30
Stephenson Way PL5: Plym 5J 11
Stibb La. PL21: Ivy 2A 24
Stillman Ct. PL4: Plym 5F 5
Stillman St. PL4: Plym 5F 5 (7D 18)
Stirling Ct. PL5: Plym 6F 11
Stirling Rd. PL5: Plym 6F 11
Stoggy La. PL7: Plymp 2G 21
(not continuous)
STOKE 1A 4 (5A 18)
Stoke Damerel Community College
Sports Cen. 4A 18
Stoke Hill La.
PL20: C'stone, Yelv 6A 38
Stoke Rd. PL1: Plym 3A 4 (6A 18)
PL8: Noss M 6G 35
Stokesay Av. PL6: Plym 2E 12
Stokes La. PL1: Plym 6F 5
Stokingway Cl. PL9: Plyms 4K 29
Stone Barton Cl. PL7: Plymp 2D 20
Stone Barton Rd. PL7: Plymp 2D 20
Stonehall Flats PL1: Plym 7K 17
Stonehedge Cl. PL21: Ivy 4E 24
STONEHOUSE 7K 17
Stonehouse Bri. PL1: Plym 7K 17
Stonehouse Creek Leisure Club 6K 17
Stonehouse St. PL1: Plym 7K 17
Stoney Lands PL12: L'ake 1C 8
Stopford Pl. PL1: Dev 5J 17
Stott Cl. PL3: Plym 3J 19
Stour Cl. PL3: Plym 2J 19
Stowe Gdns. PL5: Plym 5A 12
Stowford Bus. Pk. *PL21: Ivy 4E 24*
(off Blair Rd.)
Strand St. PL1: Plym 1K 27
Strashleigh Vw. PL21: L Mill 4K 23
Strathbrook Ter. *PL2: Plym 3J 17*
(off St Levan Rd.)
Stratton Wlk. PL2: Plym 7C 12
Stray Pk. PL8: Yeal 5B 32
Strode Rd. PL7: Plymp 2G 21
Stroma Cl. PL6: Plym 7E 6
Stroud Pk. Rd. PL2: Plym 1B 18
Stuart Rd. PL1: Plym 1A 4 (5K 17)
PL3: Plym 1A 4 (5K 17)
Sturdee Rd. PL2: Plym 3K 17
Sugar Mill Bus. Pk.
PL9: Plyms 7H 19
Summerfield Ct. PL21: Ivy 3B 24
Summerfields PL12: Salt 6K 9

A-Z Plymouth 53

SAFETY CAMERA INFORMATION

PocketGPSWorld.com's CamerAlert is a self-contained speed and red light camera warning system for SatNavs and Android or Apple iOS smartphones/tablets. Visit www.cameralert.co.uk to download.

Safety camera locations are publicised by the Safer Roads Partnership which operates them in order to encourage drivers to comply with speed limits at these sites. It is the driver's absolute responsibility to be aware of and to adhere to speed limits at all times.

By showing this safety camera information it is the intention of Geographers' A-Z Map Company Ltd., to encourage safe driving and greater awareness of speed limits and vehicle speed. Data accurate at time of printing.

Printed and bound in the United Kingdom by Gemini Press Ltd., Shoreham-by-Sea, West Sussex
Printed on materials from a sustainable source